A Life Worth Living

By the same author:

Nicky Gumbel

A Life Worth Living

Cook Ministry Resources, *a division of Cook Communications Ministries International*
Colorado Springs, Colorado / Paris, Ontario

Cook Ministry Resources is a division of Cook Communications Ministries
International (CCMI). In fulfilling its mission to encourage the acceptance of Jesus
Christ as personal Savior and to contribute to the teaching and putting into practice of His two great commandments, CCMI creates and disseminates Christian com-
munication materials and services to people throughout the world.

A Life Worth Living
by Nicky Gumbel

This edition issued by special arrangement with Kingsway Publications, Lottbridge
Drove, Eastbourne, East Sussex, England BN23 6NT. The right of Nicky Gumbel to
be identified as author of this work has been asserted by him in accordance with
the Copyright, Designs and Patents Act 1988

First published 1994,
This edition May, 2000

Study Guide © David Stone 1995

ISBN 0-7814-5258-9

10 9 8

Contents

Preface

The purpose of this book is to introduce, in a simple and practical way, a key letter in the New Testament to those who are starting the Christian life and beginning to read the Bible. It is intended to be read in conjunction with the Bible passages, either by an individual or as a group study, with one person preparing the Bible study using the book as a resource.

In *Questions of Life*, I set out the material we use in the *Alpha Course*. This course began at Holy Trinity Brompton Church in London as a course for those who do not attend church, those seeking to find out more about Christianity, and those who have recently come to faith in Jesus Christ. It is now being held worldwide.

At the end of the *Alpha Course*, people often ask, "What do I do now?" One of the things I encourage them to do is to study the letter of Philippians. The material in this book is based on a number of talks I have given on that subject.

I am so grateful to the many people who have been willing to read the text and offer constructive criticism. In particular I would like to thank Dr. Roland Werner, Preb. John Pearce, Ken Costa, Jon Soper, Helena Hird, Jo Glen, Tamsen Carter, Lulu Wells, Zilla Hawkins, Jamie Haith, and Patricia Hall. Finally, I want to thank Philippa Pearson Miles, who typed the manuscript and numerous corrections with good humor and superb efficiency.

Introduction

"In the future, scientists may be able to prolong life, but will it be worth living?" writes Nigel Hawkes in *The Times* in London. An Oxford professor claims it may be possible to prolong life for many people to the age of 115. But Nigel Hawkes is right to ask, "Will it be worth living?" Increased lifespan is of little value unless it is for a life worth living.

The apostle Paul did not see the prolonging of life as a major objective. Indeed, he regarded death as something of even greater worth (Philippians 1:21). Yet for him, Jesus Christ had made life profoundly worth living. In the letter to the Philippians, Paul writes directly and indirectly about why this is the case and how it can be for his readers as well.

In this book, we will look at some of the new things Jesus Christ brought to Paul's life and to the lives of the Philippians, which made their lives so supremely worth living. "Jesus Christ is the same yesterday and today and forever" (Hebrews 13:8). What He did for Paul and his readers He can do today for you and for me.

Before we look at this in detail, it is helpful to see the historical background into which Paul is writing and five remarkable features of this letter.

First, the *place* was remarkable. Paul chose the strategic city of Philippi for the first European "church plant" in 52 A.D. In modern times, he might have chosen Geneva, Strasbourg, Berlin, Brussels, or even London. Philippi, now a ruin in northeastern Greece, was a strategic city in the ancient world. It had the natural advantages of a productive soil. Its gold and silver mines, exhausted by the time of the Christian era, had made it a great commercial center. More importantly, the city of Philippi could not have been in a better geographic position, situated in the break of a line of hills separating Europe and Asia. It was on the high road that divided the two continents.

The city's name came from the father of Alexander the Great, Philip II of Macedonia, who fortified an old Thasian settlement in 356 B.C. in order to control the gold mines. It became part of the Roman Empire in 168 B.C. The assassins of Julius Caesar, Brutus, and Cassius were defeated here by Mark Anthony and Octavian (later the Emperor Augustus) in 42 B.C. At a time when church planting, the establishing of new churches, is increasingly seen as essential to the growth of the church, it is fascinating to see Paul's attitude in the letter towards this strategic "plant."

In another sense, all Christians find themselves in a "strategic place." All of us are surrounded by people who do not have a relationship with Jesus Christ: our family, our neighbors, our colleagues, our friends, and anyone else we bump into in the course of our everyday lives.

Second, there was a remarkable combination of *people*. One of the glorious features of the Christian faith is that it brings together, in a unique way, people of different nationality, background, race, color, sex, and age. The first person to be converted in Philippi was a wealthy woman called Lydia. "The Lord *opened her heart* to respond to Paul's message" (Acts 16:14, italics mine). Then she *opened her home* to Paul and to the Gospel. The second person to be converted was a native Greek slave girl, and the third was a middle-class Roman prison officer. They comprised an extraordinary cross section of ancient life—"the civilized world in miniature."[1] There were three different nationalities and three different layers of society demonstrating "the all-embracing faith which Jesus Christ brought."[2]

From the start, Christian families were at the heart of the church. It was the first instance in Paul's recorded ministry of whole families

"amen"

being gathered into the fold. First, Lydia and her family, and then the prison officer and his family. Again, we see a foretaste of things to come. As the nineteenth-century scholar J. B. Lightfoot put it: "Henceforth the worship of households plays an important part in the divine economy of the Church ... The family religion is the true starting-point, the surest foundation, of the religion of cities and dioceses, of nations and empires."[3]

Third, the *purpose* was remarkable. Philippians is a letter of encouragement. Paul was not correcting any doctrinal error nor berating them for their immorality. It was really a "thank-you" letter. The language is unclouded by any shadow of disappointment or displeasure. It is written quite informally. Paul does not impose his authority, as he often did, by calling himself the apostle Paul, but simply "Paul." He goes on in warm, personal, loving, and thankful words to bring encouragement to the church. Polycarp, the early Christian bishop and martyr, tells us that Paul used to boast about the Philippians all over the world. The attitude of positive encouragement is a much needed example for church leaders today.

Fourth, Paul's *pleasure* was remarkable. Joy, in all its fullness, is only found in Jesus Christ (John 15:11). The word "joy," in noun or verb form, appears sixteen times in the epistle. Paul was under house arrest in Rome, attached by three feet of chain to a Roman soldier. He was unjustly accused and awaiting trial and possible execution. Yet his joy was overflowing. Again, in our day, we need a revival of the association of joy with Christians and the church.

Fifth, the *preamble* is remarkable. Paul does not put himself above the people of Philippi in any way. One might have expected him to write, "Saint Paul to the servants of God at Philippi." Instead, he writes, "Slave Paul to the saints at Philippi." Paul regards every Christian at Philippi as a saint. "Saint" in the New Testament is a way of describing all Christians rather than a title reserved for special holy people. He adds, almost as an afterthought, the bishops and deacons. Incidentally, both terms are taken from secular use and simply mean "leaders" and "helpers." Paul did not see the church as a hierarchical structure. We need to beware of developing worldly hierarchies in the church. We are all saints, and we are all ordinary Christians. This letter is relevant to all of us.

Paul's greeting is also worth dwelling on: "Grace and peace to you from God our Father and Lord Jesus Christ." He adopts the traditional greeting of the Hellenistic world, *carem*, and changes it slightly to *charis*, meaning grace. He then adds the traditional Jewish greeting, *shalom*, meaning peace. In bringing these two words together, he effectively sums up the essence of Christianity.

Grace is the word that best describes all that God has done for us in Christ. Peace summarizes all the benefits we receive from a relationship with Christ. Grace is a huge word, covering the depth and breadth of God's love for us. The children's definition of grace is enlightening for all of us: God's Riches At Christ's Expense. And so it is that Paul's preamble ends. The Philippian readers, and we also, start to read this letter in the knowledge of the grace and peace of God.

New Heart

PHILIPPIANS 1:3-11

³I thank my God every time I remember you. ⁴In all my prayers for all of you, I always pray with joy ⁵because of your partnership in the gospel from the first day until now, ⁶being confident of this, that he who began a good work in you will carry it on to completion until the day of Christ Jesus.

⁷It is right for me to feel this way about all of you, since I have you in my heart; for whether I am in chains or defending and confirming the gospel, all of you share in God's grace with me. ⁸God can testify how I long for all of you with the affection of Christ Jesus.

⁹And this is my prayer: that your love may abound more and more in knowledge and depth of insight, ¹⁰so that you may be able to discern what is best and may be pure and blameless until the day of Christ, ¹¹filled with the fruit of righteousness that comes through Jesus Christ—to the glory and praise of God.

In November 1992, a friend of mine, Kerry Dixon, went to the Philippines with a team to work alongside the Christians there. One day, he and his team went to speak to an isolated tribe called the T'boli at Lake Sebu. This involved walking for several hours through rough terrain and mountain tracks over paddy fields and plantations. They took with them two interpreters: a Filipino pastor to translate English into Cebuano, and a T'boli member to translate from Cebuano into his own language. At about 8:00 P.M., after nightfall, word spread that the "white people" had appeared. The tribe emerged from the darkness to gather by the light of flaming torches. Kerry then spoke about Jesus through the two interpreters to this group of people who had never heard about Him. After the talk, they pushed forward a middle-aged man, blind from birth, who was well-known and respected throughout the village. If Jesus was God they wanted to see Him in action.

In the hushed silence, Kerry laid hands on the man and prayed for Jesus to heal him. He then asked if the man could see. The man replied through the interpreters that he could see flickering lights through the darkness. After Kerry prayed a second time, he could make out Kerry's outline in front of him. The third time Kerry prayed, there was no need for any interpretation—the man was jumping for joy and praising the living God, who had performed a miracle before their eyes. All fifty people present that night were converted and a new church was begun. The church there is still growing.

A HEART OF CONFIDENCE IN THE POWER OF GOD (VSS. 3-6)

The church at Philippi, like the church of T'boli, was founded by an extraordinary display of God's power. The endeavor began in 49 A.D. in utter frustration. Paul could not get into Asia or Bithynia. Every door appeared shut, but, as so often happens when circumstances seem against us, God opened up something much better. In a vision, Paul saw a man saying: "Come over to Macedonia and help us" (Acts 16:9). Paul responded by going with his companion, Silas, to Philippi. On the first Saturday that he was there, he went down to the river where there was a group of women praying. (They had probably gathered there because Philippi did not have the necessary ten Jewish men to form a synagogue.) As Paul spoke about Jesus, Lydia, a rich merchant woman, was converted and persuaded Paul to stay in her home.

While he was staying there, Paul was followed around the town by a fortune-teller, who was clearly under demonic influence as a result of her involvement in the occult, and who kept saying: "These men are servants of the Most High God, who are telling you the way to be saved" (Acts 16:17). Finally, after several days of this, Paul could take her endless repetitions no longer and turned around and said, "In the name of Jesus Christ I command you to come out of her!" (Acts 16:18). At that moment the evil spirit came out. The woman was a slave, and her owners were furious that she had lost her supernatural powers. They seized Paul and Silas and handed them over to the authorities. They whipped up the crowd against the two men. The magistrates bowed to the pressure and ordered that Paul and Silas be stripped, severely flogged, and thrown into prison.

In prison, with their feet in stocks, Paul and Silas prayed and sang hymns to God. They had seen God's power to change the direction of Lydia's life and to bring her whole family to faith. They had seen God's power in setting free a slave afflicted by an evil spirit. Now they saw God's power at work in another miraculous way: an earthquake shook the prison and every door flew open. The prison officer in charge was about to commit suicide because he thought all the prisoners had escaped and he feared the consequences. Faced with freedom, Paul chose instead to stay and to bring his jailer to Christ. When Paul assured him that the prisoners were all still there he asked: "What must I do to be saved?" This is what might be called "an evangelistic opportunity!" Paul explained what the prison officer had to do and thus he, and later his whole family, came to Christ and were baptized.

These events were so clearly supernatural that Paul saw the astonishing power of God behind the human agency of his words. It was God's power that started the church at Philippi; therefore Paul could have supreme confidence that God would complete what He had begun. This is the confidence we have if we are Christians: we have responded to God's call, and He has begun a good work in us.

> **!** Faced with freedom, Paul chose instead to stay and bring his jailer to Christ.

For the prison officer, the circumstances surrounding his conversion were extremely dramatic. Lydia would have been able to point to that extraordinary day when Paul arrived unannounced at the river as the starting point of her Christian life. Some of us know the exact day we became Christians; some of us may have experienced a dramatic conversion. However, it is quite likely that the children of the prison officer or of Lydia grew up as Christians and never knew a time when they did not have a relationship with God. It does not matter which category we fall into: if God begins a good work in us, He will carry it on to completion.

We need to retain this confidence even when life is difficult; indeed, that is the moment when we most need to exercise faith and hold on to the promises of God, confident in His power. When Paul writes that "he who began a good work in you will carry it on to completion until the day of Christ Jesus" (vs. 6), he is thinking primarily of the Philippian church. But the promise applies equally to individual Christians.

We can have this confidence for others as well as ourselves. Every true Christian who knows, loves, and follows Jesus Christ can be sure that God will bring to completion the work He has begun in them. Jesus promised His disciples eternal life (John 10:28)—a quality of life that starts now and goes on forever. We cannot have eternal life one minute and not the next. A Christian may lose a job, money, liberty, or even life, but never eternal life. Jesus added, "No one can snatch them out of my hand" (John 10:28).

The hallmark of the Christian is endurance. It is true that some profess the faith and then seem to fall away. This may be because their original profession of faith was spurious, or it could be that it was genuine and that they have backslidden and will one day return.

The first person I had the joy of leading to Christ was Henry. We had been walking in the mountains of Norway. As we were sitting on the train coming back home, we prayed together, and he gave his life to Christ. His life was changed. But after eighteen months, he started to drift as a Christian. He gave up reading the Bible and praying. He stopped going to church. He put all his Christian books up in the attic. For four years he wanted nothing to do with Christianity or Christians. Then, through a series of events, he came back to Jesus Christ. He told me afterwards that during those four years in which he had tried to give up being a Christian, he had always known that Christianity was true and that he could not get away no matter how hard he tried. If God begins a good work in someone, He will carry it on to completion.

A HEART OF COMPASSION FOR THE PEOPLE OF GOD (VSS. 7, 8)

Paul was not a "soft touch" or a doormat. He was quite capable of standing up to the Roman authorities who had wronged him. He did not simply allow them to get away with having mistreated him. He

pointed out that he and Silas were Roman citizens and that they had been illegally flogged. He demanded his rights and embarrassed the authorities. He knew how to be tough, but he also knew how to be tender.

When Paul says, "I have you in my heart" (vs. 7), he is expressing his deep love for the people of Philippi. He has already spoken of their partnership in the Gospel (vs. 5). Now he speaks of sharing in God's grace with them (vs. 7). There is such a close bond between those who work together for Jesus Christ. There is an even closer bond where one has been responsible for the conversion of the others. He says that he longs for all of them "with the affection of Christ Jesus" (vs. 8). The *King James Version* translates this, " ... how greatly I long after you all in the bowels of Jesus Christ." The original Greek word in the New Testament refers to the upper intestines, the heart, lungs, and liver—the place perceived as the source of deep emotion. "Compassion" is perhaps the nearest English equivalent. As J. B. Lightfoot put it: "His heart throbs with the heart of Christ."[4]

Paul was a man of love and compassion. This extended even to his jailer: without such love, Paul would no doubt have taken revenge on his torturer. Instead, he led him to Christ; he had the compassion of Jesus Christ. Paul Negrut, a Romanian pastor who was severely persecuted under the Ceausescu regime, is now one of the leaders of the church in Romania. He spent six months in a concentration camp and a further six months being interrogated all day, every day.

Attempts were made to kill his family by connecting the water pipes in his house to the electrical system. After the regime had fallen, he heard one day that the man who had persecuted him for six months was in the hospital dying of cancer. Paul Negrut went to visit him. The man's mother was crying and asked Paul to pray for her son. Paul Negrut laid hands on his persecutor and prayed for him. He recovered, and they have since prayed together.

The word in this verse for affection is frequently used of Jesus. The apostle Paul had Jesus' heart and Jesus' love, and this was the motivating force behind his ministry. Without love, it does not matter how doctrinally correct or how gifted we are, for Paul writes elsewhere that without love we are nothing (1 Corinthians 13). I know that at times I have tried to minister without love, and it is always disastrous. When love is abundant among us, we are able to let go of offenses against one another. When we lack love, we are apt to misunderstand every action and end up in disagreement.

We need to pray for the compassion of Jesus Christ to fill us. When I was in seminary I went through a difficult time spiritually. I had given up a job where I was paid to give my opinion and my services as an lawyer. I had also been involved in leadership in my local church. In seminary my opinion was no longer regarded as being of any value! In addition, I was no longer part of regular, active ministry. I began to feel very insecure. As I read a lot of books by scholars who were unorthodox in their beliefs and often hostile to biblical truths, I found my faith was under attack. My heart grew cold.

After I had been in seminary for two years I went to a conference where the speaker asked those involved in full-time ministry to come forward to be prayed for. He prayed that God would give us His heart for the people around us. As he prayed, I experienced God's love in my heart. I cried as I looked around at some of the other students and saw them in a new way. God opened my eyes to see that they, too, were struggling. I saw their loneliness, sadness, and fears. I suspect

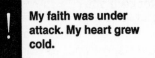

My faith was under attack. My heart grew cold.

that for a moment I had a glimpse of what Paul is speaking of here when he uses the phrase "the affection of Christ Jesus." That experience transformed my last year of seminary. I looked at people in a totally different light and I think God even opened up a ministry for me there in a small way.

A HEART OF CONCERN FOR THE PRIORITIES OF GROWTH (VSS. 9-11)

Probably eleven or twelve years had passed since Paul's original visit to Philippi. In those years the church had flourished and grown, both in numbers and in maturity. As so often is the case, the two are linked. It is not enough simply to increase in numbers. A healthy church will grow in maturity. Nor is it enough simply to grow in maturity. A healthy church should also expand in numbers. The church at Philippi had seen both types of growth. Now Paul prays for it to continue to develop.

Growth in love

First, Paul prays for growth in love. He prays that the Philippians' "love may abound more and more" (vs. 9). The Greek word means literally "overflow." Presumably he is thinking of their love for God and their love for one another. The two are inextricably linked, both in the New Testament (1 John 4:7-21) and in Christian experience. Some years ago I spent seven weeks in a church in the United States. As I mentioned earlier, my heart had grown cold, and spending seven weeks in a church full of love was like taking something out of a deep freeze and defrosting it. It was a church that loved God, and it expressed that love in worship. It was made up of people diverse in personality and background whose love for each other overflowed to us. As we were soaked in their love, our hearts were warmed.

Growth in knowledge

Second, we can see that Paul's prayer is not simply for growth in love, but that the Philippians' "love may abound more and more in knowledge and depth of insight, so that you may be able to discern what is best" (vss. 9, 10). Their love was to be more than an emotional experience; Paul prayed that it would be rooted in knowledge. Again, presumably this is both knowledge of God and of each other. English author and lexicographer Dr. Samuel Johnson once said, "The day I stop learning, I wish to die." No doubt Paul would have agreed.

A healthy Christian needs to be growing in knowledge of God. We get to know God better by spending time with Him and hearing His Spirit speak to us, primarily through the Bible and prayer. Again, our knowledge of God is linked to our knowledge of one another. We help each other to learn about God as we meet in church or in small groups. At these gatherings we also deepen our own friendships. That is why the growth of an isolated Christian is bound to be stunted, for we are meant to grow together.

In 1954 a staunch young Buddhist lay dying of tuberculosis. He was given three months to live. He was visited by an eighteen-year-old Christian, who led him to Christ, and he was miraculously healed. He went to Bible school and began to pastor a tent church in Seoul. There were five people at the first service, including himself, his sister, and an old woman who fell asleep. As they prayed and saw healings and miracles, people came to see what was happening. By 1960 the number had grown to six hundred. By 1963 there were twenty-four hundred members, by 1973 ten thousand, by 1980 a hundred thousand, and by 1982 two hundred thousand. The church now has well over six hundred thousand members. The name of that

pastor is Yonggi Cho, and he says that the key to the growth of his church lay in what they call the "home cell" groups. These small groups meet in homes where people grow in love and in knowledge of God and of one another.

Growth in holiness

Third, we see that Paul prayed for growth in holiness of life. He prays that the Philippians "may be pure and blameless until the day of Christ, filled with the fruit of righteousness that comes through Jesus Christ—to the glory and praise of God" (vss. 10, 11). The Greek word for "pure" means "unmixed." It describes an inner purity in which even our motives are unmixed. The Greek word for "blameless" means "without giving offense" and refers more to the outer way of life. So Paul prays that they may be holy both inwardly and outwardly.

The broadcaster and journalist Malcolm Muggeridge wrote of Mother Teresa:

> When I first set eyes on her … I at once realized that I was in the presence of someone of unique quality. That was not due to her appearance, which is homely and unassuming, so that words like "charm" or "charisma" do not apply. Nor to her shrewdness and quick understanding, though these are very marked; nor even to her manifest piety and true humility and ready laughter.

There is a phrase in one of the psalms that always, for me, evokes her presence: "the beauty of holiness"—that special beauty, amounting to a kind of pervasive luminosity generated by a life dedicated wholly to loving God and His creation.[5]

This kind of wholeness of life will be fruitful. Paul speaks of the "fruit of righteousness." Sin is a barrier to God's blessing, both in our individual lives and in the church. This has been seen time and time again in church history. Jonathan Goforth tells the story of what happened in Korea in 1907:

> Eight days had been set aside for prayer. On the last day there had been as yet no special manifestation of the power of God. That evening 1500 people were assembled to pray. The heavens over them seemed as brass. Was it possible that God was going to deny them the outpouring prayed for? Then they were all startled as one of the leaders stood up and said, "I am Achan. God cannot bless because of me." This man had abused his position of trust and taken $100 from a widow in the congregation. He promised to return the money in the morning.
>
> Instantly it was realized that the barriers had fallen, and that God, the Holy One, had come. Conviction of sin swept the audience. The service commenced at seven o'clock Sunday evening and did not end until two o'clock Monday morning, yet during all that time dozens were standing, weeping, awaiting their turn to confess. Day after day the people assembled now, and always it was manifest that the Refiner was in His temple ... (Sin) hindered the Almighty God while it remained covered and it glorified Him as soon as it was uncovered; and so with rare emotions did all the confessions in Korea that year.[6]

In the opening verses of Philippians we see an insight into Paul's heart. We see his faith and his complete confidence in the power of God. We see his love and compassion for the people of God. We see his hope reflected in his concern for the principles of growth. We see him looking forward to "the day of Christ." The word that appears more than any other in these first verses is "Christ." Paul's heart was a reflection of that of Jesus Christ. He had a confidence like that of Jesus in the power of God. He saw people as Jesus saw them—with the heart of God. He longed for them to grow into the likeness of Jesus—"to the glory and praise of God" (vs. 11).

2 New Purpose

PHILIPPIANS 1:12-30

[12]*Now I want you to know, brothers, that what has happened to me has really served to advance the gospel.* [13]*As a result, it has become clear throughout the whole palace guard and to everyone else that I am in chains for Christ.* [14]*Because of my chains, most of the brothers in the Lord have been encouraged to speak the word of God more courageously and fearlessly.*

[15]*It is true that some preach Christ out of envy and rivalry, but others out of goodwill.* [16]*The latter do so in love, knowing that I am put here for the defense of the gospel.* [17]*The former preach Christ out of selfish ambition, not sincerely, supposing that they can stir up trouble for me while I am in chains.* [18]*But what does it matter? The important thing is that in every way, whether from false motives or true, Christ is preached. And because of this I rejoice.*

Yes, and I will continue to rejoice, [19]*for I know that through your prayers and the help given by the Spirit of Jesus Christ, what has happened to me will turn out for my deliverance.* [20]*I eagerly expect and hope that I will in no way be ashamed, but will have sufficient courage so that now as always Christ will be exalted in my body, whether by life or by death.* [21]*For to me, to live is Christ and to die is gain.* [22]*If I am to go on living in the body, this will mean fruitful labor for me. Yet what shall I choose? I do not know!* [23]*I am torn between the two: I desire to depart and be with Christ, which is better by far;* [24]*but it is more necessary for you that I remain in the body.* [25]*Convinced of this, I know that I will remain, and I continue with all of you for your progress and joy in the faith,* [26]*so that through my being with you again your joy in Christ Jesus will overflow on account of me.*

[27]*Whatever happens, conduct yourselves in a manner worthy of the gospel of Christ. Then, whether I come and see you or only hear about you in my absence, I will know that you stand firm in one spirit, contending as one man*

for the faith of the gospel [28]*without being frightened in any way by those who oppose you. This is a sign to them that they will be destroyed, but that you will be saved—and that by God.* [29]*For it has been granted to you on behalf of Christ not only to believe on him, but also to suffer for him,* [30]*since you are going through the same struggle you saw I had, and now hear that I still have.*

Some years ago I saw a television interview with the British Ambassador in Beirut, whose embassy had been ransacked. It was chaos everywhere, but he kept that famous British stiff upper lip. He was clearly disheveled, but he had done his best to straighten himself out for the interview. He explained the ordeal they had just been through: everything of value had been stolen, his whole family had been confined to the basement, and they were living under a very real fear of attack. Threats had been made to every member of his family. They had very little food, all the services had been cut off, and there was no electricity or running water. He concluded by saying: "Life is really rather uncomfortable."

In a similar way, Paul, who describes himself as "an ambassador in chains" (Ephesians 6:20), understates his suffering. He refers to "what has happened to me" (Philippians 1:12). In reality, he had faced false accusation and mob violence. He was stripped and stretched out to be tortured. He was then put on trial, where he was illegally assaulted. He faced an assassination plot and ended up in the hands of a tyrant. He was shipwrecked on his way to Rome and was now confined in prison, uncertain about whether or when he would be executed (Acts 21-28). In writing to the Philippians, twice he alludes to all this suffering as simply "what has happened to me" (Philippians 1:12, 19).

Not only does Paul understate his suffering, he actually rejoices in it, because he sees that through it his supreme calling in life is being fulfilled. That calling can be summed up in three words: "advance the gospel" (vs. 12). The Greek word for "advance" means "advancement in spite of obstructions and dangers which would block the path of the traveller."7 This is the task that was given to Paul and is given to all Christians. In this section we see how we should go about the task and what it means in practice.

Gospel possibilities (vss. 12-14)

Word had spread about the reason for Paul's imprisonment. Paul says: "It has become clear throughout the whole palace guard and to everyone else that I am in chains for Christ" (vs. 13). The palace guard was made up of crack imperial troops. The Emperor Augustus had ten thousand specially picked troops, and Vitellius increased the number to sixteen thousand. They were paid more and given a large sum of money when they retired.

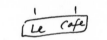

It was to these men that Paul was chained for four hours at a time. No doubt he made the most of this opportunity to tell them the Good News about Jesus Christ. He didn't say, "I can't do anything at the moment. I'll wait until I'm released." He made the most of every opportunity. He spoke to those he was able to and wrote letters to others. These letters, unknown to him, became part of the New Testament and changed the course of history.

Many Christians long to be released in order that they can tell others the Good News. They feel chained to their jobs or trapped in their homes. They look forward to a time when they need not work, or when the children have left home and they can really serve Christ. But now is the time: the possibilities are where we are. A job in the secular world is an opportunity for the Gospel. If we are bringing up children, we can take the Good News of Christ into the local community. In the very process of parenthood, we are performing a key role as we bring up "soldiers for Christ."

The opportunities are where we are. Suzanna Wesley, mother of John and Charles, had 19 children, and as a result, she and her husband were extremely poor. Her husband left home twice, once because he was put in a debtors' prison and the second time because he disagreed with his wife's political views! She educated all the children single-handedly, teaching them Greek (by the age of 10), and most importantly, the Christian faith. She rarely left her home, as she was too busy running the household, farming the land, and schooling the children. However, every day she put her apron over her head for one hour and prayed. The children knew not to disturb her during that time.

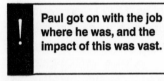

! Paul got on with the job where he was, and the impact of this was vast.

"Within the walls of her home," her biographer wrote, "she carried out a ministry to her children that was to change first England and then the world."

Suzanna Wesley explained her motivation thus: "I hope the fire I start will not only burn all of London, but all of the United Kingdom as well. I hope it will burn all over the world."

It did! She made the most of her opportunities by getting on with the job where she was.

Paul got on with the job where he was. Are we getting on with the job where we are? What are our opportunities? Are we making the most of them? It is easy to think that it is up to church leaders or professional evangelists to tell other people about Christ, but this is something we can all do at some level. Pope John Paul wrote, "I sense that the moment has come to commit all of the church's energies to a new evangelization. No believer in Christ, no institution of the Church, can avoid this supreme duty: to proclaim Christ to all peoples."

All of us can have an impact. The impact Paul had was vast. Not only did many hear about Jesus Christ directly from Paul, but also other Christians—not just the leaders but "most of the brothers" (vs. 14)—were "encouraged to speak the word of God more courageously and fearlessly" (vs. 14). This is the calling for all Christians. The first Christians saw his condition and realized that they had far less to fear. In the same way, as we read of the boldness of Christians in persecuted countries, it encourages us to speak more courageously.

I once heard a Chinese Christian, Pastor Cheng, speak at a conference. This well-educated Christian leader had spent eighteen years in a Chinese labor camp for preaching the Good News of Jesus Christ. In prison, he had been given the job of working in a human waste cesspool. It was so deep that he had to get into it in order to empty it. Because of the smell, the other prisoners and guards kept away. Pastor Cheng said that he "enjoyed the solitude … I could pray to our Lord as loud as I needed and loudly recite the scriptures and the psalms and loudly sing also the hymns." He said he had "wonderful fellowship together with our Lord … None other has known such joy … The cesspool became my private garden." I think all who heard him speak were encouraged to speak the word of God more courageously and fearlessly!

We in the West, who have the least to fear, are the most frightened. Our fears are of unpopularity or social isolation, but others have to face torture, imprisonment, and death. The time has come for the church in the West to make the most of its freedom and get on with the task of advancing the Gospel. Wherever we are, the possibilities for spreading the Good News are enormous.

GOSPEL PRIORITIES (VSS. 15-18B)

Some who were preaching the Gospel took advantage of the opportunity of Paul's imprisonment to advance their own cause. Their motives were envy, rivalry, and selfish ambition (vss. 15-17). It matters a great deal that people should hear the undistorted message of the Gospel. The message is nonnegotiable: we are not at liberty to tamper with it. Paul wrote that if anyone "should preach a gospel other than the one we preached to you, let him be eternally condemned!" (Galatians 1:8). The *means* by which we preach it also matter: the Spanish Inquisition (with its widespread use of torture) could not possibly be a legitimate way of preaching the Good News of Jesus Christ! The end does not justify the means. Paul is not speaking here about the message or the means, but about the *motives* of the preachers (vs. 18). These, he says, are secondary.

As we have seen, Paul longs for our motives to be pure. But more important than the motives of the preacher is that Christ is preached. Paul would rather that Christ were preached for false *motives* than that He was not preached at all.

Sometimes people refrain from doing what is right because they are worried about their motives. They say, "I can't become a Christian because my motives would not be right." Paul would reply that it is better to do the right thing even if the motives are mixed or wrong.

Nor should we be too harsh on others who are preaching the Gospel. Some may do it for money or self-aggrandizement. Rather than criticize them, we should rejoice, with Paul, that Christ is preached.

GOSPEL PURPOSE FOR LIVING (VSS. 19-26)

Paul says he is not remotely worried about death—so long as Jesus is honored. In many ways he regards death as "gain" (vs. 21). He writes: "I desire to depart and be with Christ, which is better by far" (vs. 23). Many Christians have felt the same. Mozart described death as "the key which unlocks the door to our true happiness." Henry Venn (1725-1797) was one of the founders of the influential group of Christian laymen known as "the Clapham sect." When the doctors told him that he was going to die in two weeks, that fact transported him into such joy and excitement that he lived an extra three months!

I read the last letters that Helmuth James, Count von Moltke, wrote to his wife and children before he died. He was the leader of the Kreisau Circle, a German resistance group during World War II, opposed to Nazism. In January 1944, he was arrested because he warned a friend of the imminence of his arrest. The following year, the People's Court condemned him to death, and the sentence was carried out on January 23, 1945. Von Moltke was then thirty-seven. In his last letters he wrote of being overpowered by "the demonstration of God's presence and omnipotence." Shortly before his death, he was severely beaten. He wrote, "I know in view of today's experience that God can also make these beatings seem as nothing, even if I should have not one sound bone left in my body when they hang me." He goes on later to quote the hymn: "And he for death is ready, who living clings to thee." Like Paul, he could say, "For to me, to live is Christ and to die is gain" (vs. 21).

Paul Negrut, the Romanian pastor I referred to in Chapter 1, said of his experiences of persecution: "The strongest weapon that the world has is to sentence you to death. After they kill you there is nothing else they can do to you. That was the lesson that I learned time and again from the secret police in Romania." Again and again they threatened him with death.

> How do you respond to that? The greatest threat and power that they have is the power to kill you. Our greatest victory is to die. So whenever they told me, "We are going to kill you," I said, "I can hardly wait. That will be my greatest victory. Because then you will lose me forever and I will be forever home. I will reach my destination—I can hardly wait."

31

Although death held no terror for Paul, he desired to go on living for the sake of others. He knew that any extension of life meant "fruitful labor" (vs. 22). He knew that it was necessary for the sake of the Philippians (vs. 24), and for their "progress and joy" (vss. 25, 26).

Paul's whole purpose in life was Christ. He says, "To me, to live is Christ" (vs. 21). This contrasts sharply with what drives so many around us today. Some are driven by the desire for money and the apparent security it brings. Others are driven by the desire to be loved or the quest for sexual satisfaction. Still others are driven by a hunger for success, fame, and significance. Madonna, for example, has said, "I won't be happy until I'm as famous as God."[8]

Others have realized that only in Jesus Christ do we find the meaning and purpose of life. The golfer Bernhard Langer said in an interview on television:

> The lifestyle we (especially us sportsmen) are leading—it is all about money and who you are and who you know and what you have, and those things aren't really the most important things. I think people who have these things, they realize that even when they have achieved all the goals they wanted to achieve and they have all the millions of pounds they wanted and all the sports cars and the places they want to go to—there is still something missing in their life. I believe that's Jesus Christ.

Paul's purpose in life was to know Christ and to make Christ known to others. For that he needed help. He needed prayer and the help of the Holy Spirit (vs. 19)—God works through both. It is neither our prayers by themselves, nor the Spirit working by Himself making our prayers superfluous, but a combination of the two working together.

GOSPEL PATTERN OF LIFE (VSS. 27-30)

It is not enough to speak the Gospel, we must also live it. Paul says: "Whatever happens, conduct yourselves in a manner worthy of the gospel of Christ" (vs. 27). The word for "conduct" means "live as citizens." Paul is using the image of citizenship that would have been familiar to his readers. Philippi was a Roman colony, and the Philippians were Roman citizens. They spoke the Roman language, wore Roman dress, and followed Roman customs; their magistrates had Roman titles, and they conducted the same ceremonies as in Rome. They were intensely proud of their privileges, which were those of Rome itself. Nowhere were people more proud of being Roman citizens than within their colonies. Their patriotism and lifestyle were similar to the British colonies in the days of the Empire.

Paul now uses this analogy. They would have wanted to live a life worthy of Rome. However, their true citizenship is now in heaven and their Christian colony on earth. They must live a life worthy of the city of heaven—a life of, among other things, freedom, love, and joy. Then others would say, "I want to be a citizen of that colony."

People are often drawn to the Gospel of Jesus Christ because of the life of another Christian. Usually interest has been aroused by the difference Christ makes to a member of the family, a friend, or a work colleague, who is living a life "worthy of the gospel" (vs. 27).

This is not only a matter of individual Christians living the Gospel out on their own; there is also a corporate aspect. Paul hopes to see that they

stand firm in one spirit, contending as one man for the faith of the gospel without being frightened in any way by those who oppose you. This is a sign to them that they will be destroyed, but that you will be saved—and that by God. For it has been granted to you on behalf of Christ not only to believe on him, but also to suffer for him, since you are going through the same struggle you saw I had, and now hear that I still have (vss. 27b-30).

Paul turns here from the image of citizens to the image of a phalanx: a formidable military device. A core of highly disciplined, heavily armed infantry stood shoulder to shoulder in files normally eight men deep. As long as they did not break rank, they were virtually invincible and struck terror into their enemies. Using this method, Philip of Macedonia had united the city-states of Greece and taken the city of Philippi.

This is a reflection of the unity that the Gospel should bring to our relationships. We are united with a common faith in a hostile world. There will be opposition (vs. 28). There will be suffering and struggling (vss. 29, 30). But we need not be frightened (vs. 28); we are not in this alone. An attack on one is an attack on all. The enemy will seek to divide us, but we must resist him and provide a united front to the world. We must fight division at all levels: as individuals, as small groups, as congregations, and as denominations. We must seek "to stand firm in one spirit" (vs. 27). Then the world will believe.

3 New Attitude

PHILIPPIANS 2:1-11

If you have any encouragement from being united with Christ, if any comfort from his love, if any fellowship with the Spirit, if any tenderness and compassion, [2]then make my joy complete by being like-minded, having the same love, being one in spirit and purpose. [3]Do nothing out of selfish ambition or vain conceit, but in humility consider others better than yourselves. [4]Each of you should look not only to your own interests, but also to the interests of others.

[5]Your attitude should be the same as that of Christ Jesus:

[6]Who, being in very nature God, did not consider equality with God something to be grasped, [7]but made himself nothing, taking the very nature of a servant, being made in human likeness. [8]And being found in appearance as a man, he humbled himself and became obedient to death—even death on a cross! [9]Therefore God exalted him to the highest place and gave him the name that is above every name, [10]that at the name of Jesus every knee should bow, in heaven and on earth and under the earth, [11]and every tongue confess that Jesus Christ is Lord, to the glory of God the Father.

So many people today look for happiness through money, sex, relationships, or success. Paul seems to have found the secret to happiness, but it is not in any of these things. He is in prison, chained to a Roman soldier, guarded, unjustly accused, with no comforts, and facing an early death. He has lost his freedom and is unable to do what he loved doing most of all: preach the Gospel. Yet he writes to say, in effect, "I am ninety-nine percent happy—my joy is almost complete" (Philippians 2:2). Only one thing will make him completely happy. We might expect him to say, "If only I could be released from prison," or, "If only these chains could be removed," or, "If only you could provide me with a comfortable bed or a basket of food!" Instead, what he asks for has nothing to do with his own needs.

Paul is concerned for the people at Philippi. There was a hint of disunity between two women called Euodia and Syntyche (Philippians 4:2). There was no great split, but Paul sees the danger signs and

knows that the devil is always trying to sow seeds of disunity. So he appeals for unity with all the passion and arguments he can muster.

First, he appeals to the Philippians' unity in Christ—"being united with Christ" (vs. 1). Literally this means "in Christ," as all Christians are "in Christ." Christ is the chief ground of our unity. The very fact that they are all Christians should be the greatest incentive for unity.

Second, he uses the argument of God's love—"if any comfort from his love" (vs. 1). If we have any experience of God's love for us, we cannot fail to love our brothers and sisters who are equally loved by God.

Third, Paul points to the unity the Holy Spirit brings—"if any fellowship with the Spirit" (vs. 1). Every Christian has the Holy Spirit living within, and He is the one who unites us.

Fourth, he appeals to Christian love—"tenderness and compassion" (vs. 1). If we love people, we will hate disunity.

So, Paul says, "make my joy complete" (vs. 2) by your unity. He urges the Philippians to a unity of mind, to be "like-minded" (vs. 2);

not necessarily agreeing about every issue (which would be unrealistic), but having the same approach and attitude. Next, he urges a unity of emotions—"having the same love" (vs. 2); not necessarily loving the same things (for everyone is different), but again having the same attitude of love. Finally, he urges a unity of wills—"one in spirit and purpose" (vs. 2); they should have the same ultimate goal, even if they cannot always agree on how exactly to get there.

WRONG ATTITUDES (VSS. 3-4)

The one thing that will destroy the unity of the Philippians is having the wrong attitude.

Selfish ambition

The first wrong attitude is "selfish ambition" (vs. 3). There is nothing wrong with ambition in itself. "Ambition is the desire to succeed. There is nothing wrong with it if it is genuinely subordinated to the will and glory of God."[9] What is wrong is *selfish* ambition. The original word used could also be translated "rivalry." Gore Vidal, who described Christianity as "the greatest disaster ever to strike the West,"[10] has said, "It is not enough to succeed. Others must fail" and, "Whenever a friend succeeds, a little something in me dies."[11] Such selfish ambition and rivalry, quite apart from the fact that they bring dissatisfaction and unhappiness, are bound to lead to disunity.

Vain conceit

The second wrong attitude is self-importance, "vain conceit" (vs. 3). The commentator William Barclay describes this as "the desire for personal prestige." He says: "Prestige is for many people an even greater temptation than wealth. To be admired and respected, to have a platform seat, to have one's opinion sought, to be known by name and appearance, even to be flattered, are for many people most desirable things."[12] I saw once that the license plate "VIP 1" was to be offered at auction and expected to sell for $150,000, presumably because so many like to consider themselves Very Important Persons! This self-importance is very unattractive, and there is a relief in seeing such people deflated. One such "VIP," who was full of his own self-importance, was irritated by what he considered to be incompetent service from his new steward at his club. "Do you know who I am?" he thundered. "No, sir," was the reply, "but I will make inquiries and then come back and let you know."

The opposite of such pomposity and pride is the "humility" that Paul urges when he says, "Consider others better than your-selves" (vs. 3). Humility does not mean we must necessarily consider everyone to be more gifted. Pete Sampras is not required to think that I am a better tennis player than he is—that would be false humility! Nor does it mean we must necessarily consider everyone as morally better than ourselves. For Mother Teresa to think Adolf Hitler was morally better than her would require mental gymnastics. We are required to think that others are more important than ourselves. This is the opposite of self-importance.

Self-centeredness

The third wrong attitude is self-centeredness: being concerned only with ourselves and our own interests. Paul says, "Each of you should look not only to your own interests, but also to the interests of others" (vs. 4). Self-centeredness is the heart of the human problem.

Martin Luther described fallen humanity as "man curved in on himself." Malcolm Muggeridge spoke of the "tiny dark dungeon of the ego." William Temple described original sin in these terms:

> I am the centre of the world I see; where the horizon is depends on where I stand ... Education may make my self-centeredness less disastrous by widening my horizon of interest; so far it is like

39

the climbing of a tower, which widens the horizon for physical vision while leaving one still the centre and standard of reference.[13]

Instead, we are urged to look to the interests of others (vs. 4). This means an attitude of love in big and little things; not only in the overall direction of our lives, but also in our everyday actions. It is about how we treat our family, our neighbors, our work colleagues, and members of the church; about what is central to our conversations, our concerns, our thoughts, our giving, and our prayers.

Philip Yancey made this observation: "In my career as a journalist, I have interviewed diverse people. Looking back, I can roughly divide them into two types: stars and servants. The stars include sporting heroes, film actors, music performers, famous authors, TV personalities, and the like. In my limited experience, these "idols" are as miserable a group of people as I have ever met. Most have troubled or broken marriages. Nearly all are hopelessly dependent on psychotherapy. In a heavy irony, these larger-than-life heroes seem tormented by incurable self-doubt.

I have also spent time with servants. People like Dr. Paul Brant, who worked for 20 years among the poorest of the poor, leprosy patients in rural India . . . or relief workers in Somalia, Sudan, Ethiopia, Bangladesh, or other such repositories of human suffering. I was prepared to honor and admire these servants, to hold them up as inspiring examples. . . . I was not, however, prepared to envy them.

But as I now reflect on the two groups side by side, stars and servants, the servants clearly emerge as the favored ones. They work for low pay, long hours, and no applause, "wasting" their talents and skills among the poor and uneducated. But somehow in the process of losing their lives they have found them."

What a challenging statement that is: as we "waste" our lives on other people, we will find meaning of life. It seems to echo the words of Jesus Himself, who gave us the command to "love your neighbor as yourself."

I once tried to explain to a small group of nonchurchgoers that the commands of Jesus were not just negative—"thou shalt not"— but also positive. Jesus summed up the two great commandments as: "Love the Lord your God with all your heart and with all your soul and with all your strength and with all your mind," and, "Love your neighbor as yourself" (Luke 10:27). One of the people in the group replied, "Well, you don't know my neighbor!" That is the point. When Jesus gave the command, He was well aware of the shortcomings and imperfections of humankind. He also knew all about our innate self-centeredness, and yet He knew that within the two great commandments of love lay the key to life lived in all its fullness.

RIGHT ATTITUDES (VSS. 5-11)

I keep a notebook of my prayers and thoughts with "Private and Confidential" written on the outside. Although I doubt anyone would be interested in my thoughts, in many cases it would be fascinating to read another person's private and confidential thoughts to see what is going on in that person's mind. In this passage we get a glimpse into the mind of Jesus Christ.

We see that in His mind there was no selfish ambition or self-importance or self-centeredness; rather we see the opposite. In one of the greatest passages in the New Testament, which was probably an early Christian hymn, we see the attitude of Jesus Christ, which Paul says should be ours as well.

First, Jesus let go of His *natural* status. Jesus was "in very nature God" (vs. 6). His status was no less than God Himself, yet He "did not consider equality with God something to be grasped" (vs. 6). You only have to go to a one-day sale to see "grasping" in practice.

The act of grasping is a contradiction to Jesus' attitude to life. Instead of climbing up the ladder of achievement, Jesus climbed down it. He demoted Himself. He became downwardly mobile. He became a man. The incarnation is the opposite of selfish ambition: not the story of "rags to riches," but the reverse. Jesus started at the top and went right down to the bottom, quite deliberately, because He was ambitious not for Himself, but for God and for us, and He set out to achieve His ambition.

Second, Jesus let go His *social* status. Jesus could not have started with a higher social position. He was equal with God (vs. 6). He was the King of kings and Lord of lords, and yet He "made himself nothing" (vs. 7), taking the very nature of a servant (literally, a slave). This is the reverse of social climbing; Jesus climbed down the social ladder and demoted Himself to become a slave. "The Son of Man did not come to be served, but to serve" (Mark 10:45).

Third, Jesus let go His *legal* status, humbling Himself still further (vs. 8). He gave us His right to life "and became obedient to death—even death on a cross" (vs. 8). Had He been self-centered and looking after His own interests, He would never have died. He died as a criminal on a Roman gibbet, tortured to death in a most ignominious way. It was a death reserved for the lowest order of society—the slave class. He was giving His life as a "ransom for many" (Mark 10:45). He became like us so that we might become like Him; became a slave so that we might go free; died that we might have life.

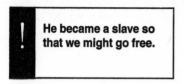

He became a slave so that we might go free.

Jesus went from the light of God to the darkness of death; from the highest height to the deepest depth. Paul says that our attitude should be the same as that of Christ Jesus. We cannot repeat what Jesus did for us on the Cross. However, we are called to give up our selfish ambitions, self-importance, and self-centeredness and give ourselves to downward mobility, humble service, and unselfish love.

Perhaps a better translation of verse five is: "Have this mind among yourselves which is yours in Christ Jesus." In other words, Paul is saying that this attitude is already ours as Christians. As Alec Motyer pointed out, "The great glory of Christian ethics is that it calls us to be what we are."[14] In Christ, we already have His attitude and His example, and we are called to follow Him.

Some years ago, I went to a cricket match at Hove county ground. I saw there a small boy with an adult cricket bat cut down to a third of its size. He was practicing in the nets at the side of the ground. He walked up to the wicket with great confidence and started to hit a

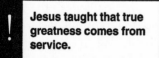

Jesus taught that true greatness comes from service.

tennis ball all over the place with great power and timing. There was quite a crowd watching. I discovered the boy was Jamie Parker, the son of Paul Parker, who played cricket for England and was then Captain of Sussex. Jamie's ability was inherited, and he had also clearly benefited from the example of his father. But he still had to practice.

So it is with our attitude: we have inherited God's blessing, as co-heirs of Christ, and we have the example of Jesus to follow, yet it still takes a lifetime even to approximate the standard Jesus set for us.

This may not be the path of true greatness in the eyes of men and women, but it is in the eyes of God. "Therefore God exalted him to the highest place and gave him the name that is above every name, that at the name of Jesus every knee should bow, in heaven and on earth and under the earth, and every tongue confess that Jesus Christ is Lord, to the glory of God the Father" (vss. 9-11). Jesus Himself taught that true greatness comes from service. He said: "Whoever wants to become great among you must be your servant, and whoever wants to be first must be slave of all" (Mark 10:43, 44). He taught that humility leads to exaltation. He said: "For everyone who exalts himself will be humbled, and he who humbles himself will be exalted" (Luke 14:11). We cannot exalt ourselves. If we try to, God promises to humble us. This is the extraordinary paradox of the Christian life. Jesus' disciples took some time to learn this principle, but they did learn it in the end. Peter writes that we should clothe ourselves with humility towards one another because "God opposes the proud but gives grace to the humble. Humble yourselves, therefore, under God's mighty hand, that he may lift you up in due time" (1 Peter 5:5-6). Now Paul tells us that this principle, taught by Jesus and learned by His disciples, was fulfilled supremely in Jesus' own life. He humbled Himself to the lowest position, and God exalted Him to the "highest place"—where the whole church, indeed the whole cosmos, is under His authority (vs. 10).

God has given Jesus a new name. The first creed of the early

Christian church was "Jesus Christ is Lord" (vs. 11). He is Lord, not just in the sense of owner or master, or even in the sense that was used of the Roman emperors, but in the same sense as God the Father is Lord. Indeed, "Lord" was the way in which God's name in the Old Testament was translated in the Greek version of the Hebrew Scriptures. Yet there is no rivalry within the Trinity. Rather, the lordship of Jesus Christ brings glory to God the Father (vs. 11).

The first creed of the early Christian church was "Jesus Christ is Lord."

We too can bring glory to God by following the example of Jesus. We are called to love as He loved; to give up our selfish ambitions and to serve instead; to give up our self-importance and to look to the interests of others; to give up our self-centeredness and to center our lives on Jesus and on other people. We are called to become not stars, but servants.

That is why Paul could say that he was ninety-nine percent happy. He had given up selfish ambitions; it did not matter that he had lost his freedom to achieve anything for himself. He had given up self-importance, so it did not matter that he had ended up as a prisoner in chains. He had given up self-centeredness, so that he was not worried by his own conditions. He was far more worried about the interests of the Philippians. He was following the example of Jesus Christ. God exalted him to be the single greatest influence, apart from Jesus, in the astonishing and continuing spread of Christianity, bringing life, hope, and peace to countless millions of people.

4 New Responsibilities

PHILIPPIANS 2:12-18

[12]Therefore, my dear friends, as you have always obeyed—not only in my presence, but now much more in my absence—continue to work out your salvation with fear and trembling, [13]for it is God who works in you to will and to act according to his good purpose.

[14]Do everything without complaining or arguing, [15]so that you may become blameless and pure, children of God without fault in a crooked and depraved generation, in which you shine like stars in the universe [16]as you hold out the word of life—in order that I may boast on the day of Christ that I did not run or labor for nothing. [17]But even if I am being poured out like a drink offering on the sacrifice and service coming from your faith, I am glad and rejoice with all of you. [18]So you too should be glad and rejoice with me.

Paul, in a pointed application of the example of Jesus Christ in Philippians 2:6-11, urges the Philippians to take responsibility for their lives and a responsible attitude to society, making it quite clear that he takes his own responsibilities very seriously indeed.

Many in our society are unwilling to take responsibility for their actions. There is an increasing tendency to try to shift responsibility and blame to the government, the economy, the environment, employers, doctors, parents, husbands, or wives.

This refusal to take responsibility goes back to the time when Adam sinned. Adam refused to take responsibility for his actions. He blamed his wife. Eve refused to take responsibility for her actions. She blamed the devil. But, ultimately, whatever the mitigating circumstances, we are all accountable for our actions and our lives.

OUR RESPONSIBILITY FOR OUR OWN LIVES (VSS. **12, 13**)

Every Christian must take responsibility for his or her life. Paul urges the Christians at Philippi, "Therefore, my dear friends, as you have always obeyed—not only in my presence, but now much more in my absence—continue to work out your salvation with fear and trembling, for it is God who works in you to will and to act according to his good purpose" (vss. 12, 13).

Paul links this section to the last by the word "therefore." It is because Jesus has set an example of obedience in working out His responsibility that we are to follow that example and to "work out" our "salvation" (vs. 12). Indeed, that is the only appropriate response to Jesus' sacrifice on our behalf.

"Salvation" is, perhaps, the most important word in the New Testament. "For those who find 'salvation' a bit of meaningless religious jargon, and even an embarrassment, 'freedom' is an excellent substitute."[15] To be saved by Jesus Christ is to be set free. Jesus sets us free from our guilt, our addictions, and our fear of death (and with that from all other fears). He sets us free to know God, to love others, and "to be our true selves, as God made us and meant us to be."[16]

Freedom and responsibility go hand in hand. As George Bernard Shaw put it, "Liberty means responsibility. That is why most men dread it."[17] We all have free will and are therefore responsible for our actions. Christians enjoy an even greater freedom: "the glorious freedom of the children of God" (Romans 8:21). With this greater freedom comes greater responsibility.

Paul tells us that we are to "work out" our freedom. This is different from working *for* our freedom. It is not "an objective yet to be reached" or "a benefit to be merited," but rather it is "a possession to be explored and enjoyed ever more fully." Our freedom is to be worked out just as "marriage has to be worked out. Marriage once possessed is possessed in full but merits a life time of exploration, enjoyment, development and discovery."[18] So our freedom is already possessed to the full, but we need to work it out day by day.

In particular, we need to work out the path along which we are to walk in response to God's call and the sphere of our Christian service. Each person has a different calling. For some it will be along the lines of ministry with the poor. For others it will be evangelism, for others healing, for others a prophetic ministry or teaching, or some other area. It is our responsibility to discover our gifts and to use them.

I read the obituary of George Hoffman, who founded TEAR Fund, a British relief and development organization. As its director, Hoffman guided its fortunes for its first twenty-one years. He saw its first year's income of $50,000 grow to over $20 million before he moved on. He captured the ideals of a whole generation whose eyes were opened to the dimension of tragedy on a global scale: famine, flood, earthquake, and a massive refugee problem. The obituary said: "His face could move from pain and horror to humour in a few seconds. His voice could be strong, gentle, full of passionate intensity and yet the underlying Merseyside wit was never absent ... it was a recipe which caught the attention of thousands of Christian people and turned their minds to the alleviating of human need across the world."[19] Here was a man who took responsibility seriously and worked out his freedom for God's glory.

We are to work out our freedom with "fear and trembling" (vs. 12). Such is the importance of this that we cannot take it lightly, or we risk offending God and wasting our lives. It is possible to have a saved soul and a wasted life.

Alan Redpath, the Christian writer and preacher, was once an accountant. He had given his life to God, but he still had other gods. He went to church, but his Christianity was just one compartment in his life. One day he was talking to a friend who said, "You know it is possible to have a saved soul and a wasted life." He tried to brush it off, but the words kept ringing in his ears. All week as he worked, the words came back to him like a record that had got stuck—"saved soul, wasted life." Every song on the radio seemed to be playing the same tune. On Saturday, as he played rugby, the words were still ringing in his ears. On the train home after the match the wheels of the train churned out "saved soul, wasted life." That evening the dance band seemed to be playing only one tune—"saved soul, wasted life." Eventually, he gave in to the Lord and said, in effect, "You can have all of my life." Through his ministry, many came into a relationship with Jesus Christ and had their lives changed.

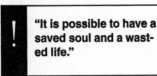

! "It is possible to have a saved soul and a wasted life."

We will not all enter full-time Christian ministry. For most, our new-found freedom will be worked out in the office, in business, in the factory, in the hospital, school, or home. Each of us has a responsibility before God to work out what He is calling us to do and then to do it for His glory.

There is a very careful balance in Paul's wording of this sentence.

We are to "work out" our salvation because it is God who "works in" us. Our newfound freedom is a gift from God, and even in the working out of it we need His help. No sin can be conquered nor anything of lasting worth accomplished without His help. We have to cooperate with the Spirit of God in all that we do. In gardening the growth comes from the plant itself, but the gardener has a vital role to play. So it is with our spiritual lives. God gives the growth, but we must tend the plant.

God's work in us includes our wills. He works in us "to will and to act according to his good purpose" (vs. 13). Many fear to trust God with their futures because they fear God will make them do something they have no desire to do, or that He will make a mess of their lives. Of course, both of these fears are without foundation. If our wills are surrendered to His will, God will give us the desire to do whatever He is calling us to do. If He calls to a ministry with the poor, that is where the person's heart will be. If He calls us to a teaching work, He will give a desire to teach. If we surrender to His will, He will work out "his *good* purpose." What He wants for our lives is good. It will not necessarily be easy, but we will not be able to improve on His plan. In fact, working out our salvation means fulfilling our potential as the whole person we were created to be.

OUR RESPONSIBILITY TO SOCIETY (VSS. 14-16A)

The New Testament speaks not so much of society's responsibility for us, but of our responsibility for those around us. We live in a "crooked and depraved generation" (vs. 15). The word for "crooked" suggests that it is distorted in its values. This is true not just of Paul's generation, but of ours, and of every other generation. It is no good looking back on the "good old days." We are now living in "the good old days" of the future.

Here are two descriptions of young people in society:

> I see no hope for the future of our people if they are dependent on the frivolous youth of today, for certainly all youth are reckless beyond words. … When I was young we were taught to be discreet and respectful of elders, but the present youth are exceedingly impatient of restraint.

> The children now love luxury; they show disrespect for elders and love chatter in the place of exercise. Children are tyrants, not the servants of their households. They no longer rise when their elders enter the room. They contradict their parents, chatter before company, gobble up dainties at the table, cross their legs and tyrannize their teachers.[20]

The first description is taken from Hesiod, a Greek poet of the eighth century B.C. The second comes from Socrates (469-399 B.C.) Not much has changed over time!

In the midst of a society warped and distorted due to its rebellion against God, Christians are called to live lives that are noticeably different from those around them. We are called to "do everything without complaining or arguing" (vs.14). The word for arguing refers to an "intellectual rebellion against God."[21] The word for complaining refers more to a moral rebellion against God. In the Greek text it is an onomatopoeic word. Perhaps the best English translation would be "murmuring," which also conjures up the sound made by those who are grumbling. It is a word used in Exodus 15:24 and Exodus 16:7 of the people of Israel. The people of Israel had received great blessing, and yet a few days later they were murmuring. It is the attitude that says, "Poor me!" and "It's not fair!" It is an attitude of self-pity.

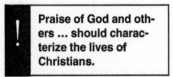

Praise of God and others … should characterize the lives of Christians.

52

Both attitudes—complaining and arguing—are the opposite of praise, which is the "fruit of lips" that confess the name of Jesus (Hebrews 13:15). Praise of God and others, rather than complaining and arguing, should characterize the lives of Christians, so that we "may become blameless and pure, children of God " (vs. 15).

The word for blameless means living a life with which no one can find fault. As the law must not only be just but must be seen to be just, so the Christian must not only be pure, but the purity of his life must be seen by all. The word used for pure means unadulterated in the way that we speak of "pure gold." This is how the children of God are supposed to live, bearing the family likeness of their Father.

As we live like this we will be in sharp contrast to the world around us. We will "shine like stars in the universe"(vs. 15). Our lifestyle should be a shining example to the world. But our responsibility involves not just our lifestyle, but also our lips.

We have a responsibility to "hold out the word of life" (vs. 16) to a society desperately needing God. A few years ago a report in the paper was headed: "Midlife fear hits men in thirties." It read:

> Men are reaching their midlife crisis earlier in life, as they achieve their goals in their thirties rather than in their forties, marriage guidance experts say. In the past men would seek satisfaction with a career change, but today the recession means many will seek comfort in an affair. Renate Olins, the director of London Marriage Guidance, said that men in their thirties reached a point which they thought would be the pinnacle of their success, only to find they were unsatisfied.[22]

We are surrounded by dissatisfied people because they have never found the relationship with God for which they were made. The Good News of Jesus Christ not only tells of life, but it also imparts life to those who hear and respond in faith. It is both our responsibility and our privilege to hold out this message to the society around us.

OUR RESPONSIBILITY TO THE CHURCH (VSS. 16B-18)

We see also in this passage how seriously Paul takes his own responsibilities. His care and concern for the Christians at Philippi are an example to us of how we should view our responsibilities towards the church and our Christian friends, for that is how Paul sees them (vs. 12). He uses two vivid illustrations.

First, Paul uses an illustration from the world of athletics. He says that he wants to be able to boast on "the day of Christ" that he "did not run or labor for nothing" (vs. 16). The word he uses for labor is probably a continuation of the same metaphor as running and refers to the training for the athletic games. In the Greek world there were the Isthmian games at Corinth, the Pan-Ionian games at Ephesus, and the Olympic games. The training for these games involved a rigorous regime. Paul saw his efforts on behalf of the Philippians in these terms. He needed to be in peak condition spiritually. He need-

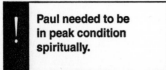

Paul needed to be in peak condition spiritually.

ed "to run" and "to labor" on their behalf because he does not want his efforts to be wasted. There is no greater disappointment than seeing our efforts to nurture new Christians come to nothing if they fall away, and no greater joy than seeing the fruit of our running and toiling in those who grow in their love and service for the Lord.

The second image that Paul uses is even stronger: it is one of sacrifice. He speaks of being "poured out like a drink offering on the sacrifice and service coming from your faith" (vs. 17). The background to this image is probably heathen sacrifice. Paul is writing to converted heathens, and he uses a picture with which they would be familiar. The "drink offering" was the cup of wine poured out as a sacrifice to the gods, accompanying a larger sacrifice. It was, therefore, a small thing that brought the major sacrifice to completion.

Paul regarded the faith and priestly service of the Philippians as a sacrifice offered to God. The language he uses is priestly. In the New Testament, every believer is a priest. The priesthood is no longer confined to a select group or tribe. All the Christians at Philippi are priests. Their faith, and the good deeds that spring out of their faith, are the sacrifice.

Such is Paul's love and sense of responsibility for the Philippians that he is willing to pour out his life before God for their sake, even if that means his own death. Indeed, he says he would be glad and rejoice if that were the case, and so should they (vs. 18). Ministry is pouring out ourselves for others.

In Libby Purves's book, *Holy Smoke*, she devotes a chapter to her encounters with various Christians. She writes this, "Even more unforgettable was Jackie Pullinger, a radical young Christian musician who set off across the world with a Quixotic naivete to find where she was called to work. She lighted upon Hong Kong's walled city of Kowloon, the 'City of darkness,' before that unspeakable slum was pulled down in 1989. In this place of misery, of violence, of prostitutes from 10 to 70 years old, of almost universal drug addiction and Triad gangs, she walked the dark alleys seeing 'another city in its place, ablaze with light. It was my dream. No more crying, no more death or pain.'"

Jackie's heart went out to the people she met, and she simply prayed for them—that they would be set free from drug addiction or from lifestyles of prostitution. Gradually, she established "houses" for the addicts and prostitutes, and thousands have left those houses with their dark lives transformed by the light of Christ.

Libby Purves goes on, "I was wary when I met her. But the evidence of her work won me over, and more than that, I like the Humpty Dumpty inversion of commonsense which marked her brand of Christianity.

"She looked at me gently, this skinny straw-haired flame of a woman, when I asked her about the sacrifice she has made. 'No sacrifice. That's dumb. I have more fun than most people. People are always telling me to take it easy or I'll burn out, but a couple of years later it always turns out that they've burned out themselves, and I haven't. The Bible doesn't say anything about looking after yourself, does it?' Unreasonable, incomprehensible in the world's terms, infuriating, glorious, Christian, all the way."

5 New Friendships

PHILIPPIANS 2:19-30

19I hope in the Lord Jesus to send Timothy to you soon, that I also may be cheered when I receive news about you. 20I have no one else like him, who takes a genuine interest in your welfare. 21For everyone looks out for his own interests, not those of Jesus Christ. 22But you know that Timothy has proved himself, because as a son with his father he has served with me in the work of the gospel. 23I hope, therefore, to send him as soon as I see how things go with me. 24And I am confident in the Lord that I myself will come soon.

25But I think it is necessary to send back to you Epaphroditus, my brother, fellow worker and fellow soldier, who is also your messenger, whom you sent to take care of my needs. 26For he longs for all of you and is distressed because you heard he was ill. 27Indeed he was ill, and almost died. But God had mercy on him, and not on him only but also on me, to spare me sorrow upon sorrow. 28Therefore I am all the more eager to send him, so that when you see him again you may be glad and I may have less anxiety. 29Welcome him in the Lord with great joy, and honor men like him, 30because he almost died for the work of Christ, risking his life to make up for the help you could not give me.

A woman who had become a Christian wrote to me: "It is such a joy to have Jesus as a friend, as His friends become your friends too, to share one's joys, laughter, and problems, which then distill hope, faith, and happiness." In today's world, friendship does not have the high value it once had. C. S. Lewis wrote:

> To the Ancients, Friendship seemed the happiest and most fully human of all loves; the crown of life and the school of virtue. The modern world, in comparison, ignores it ... It is something quite marginal; not a main course in life's banquet; a diversion; some-

thing that fills up the chinks of one's time. How has this come about? ... few value it because few experience it ... we can live

and breed without friendship. The species, biologically considered, has no need of it. [Some] may even dislike and distrust it.[23]

Yet friendship is at the heart of Christianity, and it should be at the heart of church life. Men and women were created to live in a relationship of friendship with God. This is pictured in Genesis 3 as God's desire to walk with Adam and Eve "in the garden in the cool of the day" (Genesis 3:8). It was His intention that all men and women should be described, like Moses, as friends of God.

The creation order involved not just friendship with God but friendship with one another. God said, "It is not good for the man to be alone" (Genesis 2:18). Marriage was part of God's solution—"I will make a helper suitable for him"—but human friendship, vital also in marriage, was also a crucial part of His solution.

It was the sin of Adam and Eve that caused the breakdown of their friendship, not only with God but also with each other (Genesis 3:8 and following). Since that moment, men and women have lived with the tension that we both desire and need close human friendships (because that is how we were created), and yet we find those friendships hard (because of the inherent sin in us and in the world around us). We are like two porcupines in the winter, drawing close for warmth and then spiking each other and moving apart again.

On the cross, Jesus destroyed the barrier between us and God, and also the barrier between people by destroying "the dividing wall of hostility" (Ephesians 2:14). Restored friendship is part of Jesus' redemptive work on the cross. He also set us an example of friendship. He was fully human and, like all human beings, he needed friends, both male and female. He described His chosen disciples as "friends" (John 15:14). Within that group He had a small group of three friends with whom He was especially close, one of whom was His closest friend. He demonstrated that marriage is not the only solution to "aloneness." Close friendship is another solution. Our society, with its overemphasis on sexual relationships, often undervalues this God-given provision.

In one respect, friendship is even more important than marriage. Marriage is only a temporary solution, as there will be no marriage in heaven (Matthew 22:30). Friendship can be eternal: part of heaven will be getting to know one another (including wives and husbands) better and better.

In Philippians 2:19-30, we get a fascinating insight into two of Paul's friendships. We see him as a man of flesh and blood relating in a human situation of universal interest to other men of flesh and blood. Here are three ordinary Christians who show us a model of an extraordinary relationship. We see here four marks of Christian friendship.

GENUINE INTEREST

Timothy came from Derbe or Lystra. His mother was called Eunice and was a Jewess (2 Timothy 1:5). His grandmother was called Lois. His father was a Greek. Timothy had been brought up as a Greek and was, therefore, uncircumcised. It was through Paul that Timothy had become a Christian—he was Paul's "son" in the Lord. Paul describes him as "my son whom I love" (1 Corinthians 4:17), and they had become very close friends.

They had been through a great deal together. Timothy often accompanied Paul on his travels (Acts 18:5; 20:4), including his journey to Philippi (Acts 16). Timothy had spent time in prison with Paul (Colossians 1:1; Philippians 1:1). He was associated with Paul in several of his letters (1 and I2 Thessalonians, I2 Corinthians, Colossians, Philippians). When Paul wished to send information, advice, or encouragement he often sent Timothy (Philippians 2:19, 23; 1 Thessalonians 3:6; 1 Corinthians 4:17; 16:10). Timothy was always loyal to Paul and was totally reliable (1 Corinthians 4:17).

Here Paul pays tribute to his friend. He says, "I have no one else like him, who takes a *genuine interest* in your welfare" (vs. 20, italics mine). As Paul looks around he sees the blight of self-interest, saying, "Everyone looks out for his own interests" (Philippians 2:21).

 Christian friendship arises out of a genuine love for other people.

The New York Telephone Company made a detailed study of telephone conversations to find out which word was most frequently used. They found it was the personal pronoun "I." It was used 3,990 times in five hundred telephone conversations. W. E. Gladstone once said, "Selfishness is the greatest curse of the human race."[24]

Paul chose as his friends two men who were quite different from those around him. He loved Timothy, who took "a genuine interest"

in others. He also loved Epaphroditus and says that his death would have caused him great sorrow (vs. 27). He is ungrudging in his praise of Epaphroditus (vss. 25-27) and shows a genuine concern for his safety (vs. 28). Epaphroditus himself was a loyal friend both to Paul and the Philippians. True character comes across in the big and little things, and often it is the little things that are most telling. Epaphroditus revealed his true colors in his attitude towards his fellow Philippians. Having become seriously ill, almost to the point of dying, he is troubled, not about being ill and close to death, but that they might have been upset by it. He was "distressed because you heard he was ill" (vs. 26). He was like those who, when ill, are not so much worried by the illness as the fact that they might be a burden to their family or friends.

Here we see the first mark of Christian friendship: it arises out of a genuine love for other people. Those who are only interested in themselves seldom make many friends. Those who want friends in order to satisfy a selfish requirement will never make them. Friendship comes through a genuine interest in other people. Dale Carnegie, who wrote *How to Win Friends and Influence People*, said, "You can make more friends in two months by becoming interested in other people than you can in two years by trying to get other people interested in you."[25]

Genuine love for others should not be confined to those who are already Christians. Friendship is by far the most effective way to pass on the good news of Jesus Christ. We do not make friends in order to evangelize, but friendship and evangelism go hand in hand. We make friends because we are genuinely interested in others, and because we are interested in others we want to tell them about Jesus.

COMMON FOCUS

The second reason for Paul's close friendships with Timothy and Epaphroditus was their common concern for the interests of Jesus

Christ, which were quite unlike the interests of those around them (vs. 21). Ordinary friendships are made by people with interests in common, doing things together. That is why C. S. Lewis points out:

> We picture lovers face to face but Friends side by side: their eyes look ahead ... that is why those ... people who simply "want friends" can never make any. The very condition of having Friends is that we should want something else besides Friends ... Friendship must be about something, even if it were only an enthusiasm for dominoes or white mice.[26]

Christian friendship is in a different league. It goes way beyond sharing an interest in dominoes or anything else. There is a totally different dimension to the friendship between Christians—an unparalleled closeness the New Testament calls "fellowship"—about which the world knows nothing. It results not only from our common interests, but from the trust, security, and openness arising out of our common focus on Jesus Christ.

One woman said to me, "The friendships I have made since I have become a Christian (eighteen months earlier) have been far closer and deeper than those with people I have known for thirty years." Paul, in searching for ways to describe this closeness, uses the word "brother." He describes Epaphroditus as a brother (vs. 25).

Elsewhere he describes Timothy as a brother (1 Thessalonians 3:2).

Jesus accepted everyone, but He *chose* His friends. If Jesus needed a small group of friends, so do we. We need to be able to talk with those in whom our trust runs very deep, to encourage and pray for one another. Christian friendships are extraordinarily powerful. They are enriching, rewarding, and emotionally restoring: "a main course in life's banquet."

SERVING TOGETHER

Christian friendship arises out of a common vision and goal for our lives. Paul and Timothy served together "in the work of the gospel" (vs. 22). Timothy ungrudgingly accepted second place so long as he could serve. Paul did not lord it over Timothy. He regarded him as a "co-slave" (the Greek means "he slaved with me"—vs. 22). Likewise, Epaphroditus was a "fellow-worker"(vs. 25). So often it is working together for the Gospel that brings us close to our Christian friends. Fellowship and mission go hand in hand in the New Testament. It is important to meet with other Christians simply to be together, to talk, and to pray, but if that ever becomes an end in itself, it is self-defeating. Unless we are involved together in "the work of the gospel" such groups become inward looking and eventually shrivel and die.

Conversely, as we work together, our friendships flourish and blossom. As different denominations work side by side, unity grows. We can only achieve unity by working together to bring the Good News of Jesus to those outside the church. It is then, writes Lesslie Newbigin in *The Household of God* that, "the stark contrast between Christ and no-Christ is constantly being faced. In such a situation, other matters necessarily fall into second place. The reality of what Christians have in common is seen to be of an importance far outweighing everything that divides Christians one from another."

Those in training for full-time church work are often advised that an assistant pastor should not be friends with the pastor or the congregation! How far we have moved from the New Testament model. Paul regarded both his assistant, Timothy, and his congregation, the Philippians (vs. 12), as his friends. Indeed, that surely is the only real basis for a flourishing church—close friendships among the leaders, between the leaders and congregation, and among the congregation as we all serve together "in the work of the gospel."

RISKS AND BATTLES

Paul describes Epaphroditus as a "brother, fellow-worker and *fellow-soldier*" (vs. 25, italics mine). "The three words are arranged in an ascending scale; common sympathy, common work, common danger and toil and suffering."[27]

The Christian life is not all easy. We are fellow soldiers. The battles we face may not be as severe as those of the early church. We, in the West, do not face prison, torture, and death, but nevertheless we face very real opposition. Genuine Christian faith is often despised and ridiculed. Christian friendship means supporting one another in the battles of life.

Epaphroditus had been prepared to "risk his life" for the sake of his friend Paul. His name suggests that his parents had devoted him to the service of Aphrodite—the goddess of love and also the patron of gambling! Plutarch tells us that the highest cast of the dice is called "Epaphroditus." His name may mean "one blessed with gambling luck."

Whether or not that is true, it certainly was true that Epaphroditus had the character of a gambler. The expression used in verse 30 could be translated "hazarding his life" (*Revised Standard Version*), but is more accurately translated as "gambling his life." It may have been that by associating himself with Paul, who was in prison on a capital charge, Epaphroditus risked the same charge. Or it may be that he risked draining his life by excessive hard work and disregard for his own health. Whichever it was, or whether it was a combination of the two, Epaphroditus showed reckless courage on behalf of Paul. This is the mark of true friendship. Paul himself and Barnabas are described in Acts as "men who have risked their lives for the name of our Lord Jesus Christ" (Acts 15:26).

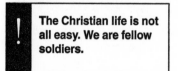

The Christian life is not all easy. We are fellow soldiers.

In the days of the early church, there was an association of men and women called "the gamblers." Their aim was to visit prisons and those sick with dangerous and infectious diseases. They were willing to hazard their lives for Jesus and for others.

I recently read a story written by a doctor in the U.S. about a girl who was suffering from a serious disease, whose only chance of recovery was through a blood transfusion from her five-year-old brother, who had miraculously survived the same disease and developed the necessary antibodies. The five-year-old agreed that he would give blood, and the transfusion took place. After this, the boy asked the doctor with a trembling voice, "Will I start to die right away?"

The doctor immediately explained that he was not about to die, but he was so impressed by the boy's courage that he asked him why he had been willing to risk his life. The boy replied, "She's my sister and I love her." When talking about His friendship with His disciples Jesus said, "Greater love has no one than this, that he lay down his life for his friends" (John 15:13).

In Shakespeare's *The Merchant of Venice*, Portia, the rich and beautiful heiress, has many suitors. Her father designs a test for them. He puts out three caskets—one of gold, one of silver, and one of lead. One of them contains a portrait of Portia. The suitor who chooses that casket will win her hand in marriage. On the gold casket are the words, "Who chooseth me shall gain what many men desire." On the silver, "Who chooseth me shall get as much as he deserves," and on the lead, "Who chooseth me must give and hazard all he hath."

The Prince of Morocco, who is full of selfish ambition and self-interest, chooses the gold and finds inside the immortal words:

> All that glisters is not gold;
> Often have you heard that told:
> Many a man his life hath sold,
> But my outside to behold.

The Prince of Arragon, who is full of self-importance, says, "I will assume desert," and opens the silver. He finds a portrait of a blinking idiot and says:

> With one fool's head I came to woo,
> But I go away with two.

Bassanio, whom Portia loves and who genuinely loves Portia, opens the lead casket and finds Portia's picture and the words:

> Turn you where your lady is
> And claim her with a loving kiss.

He is the only one of the three prepared "to give and hazard all he hath."

All friendship involves taking risks. Jesus made Himself vulnerable to His friends. He was totally open with them. He said, "I have called you friends, for everything that I learned from my Father I have made known to you" (John 15:15). Yet, in the end, He was betrayed by one of them, deserted by the others, and disowned as an embarrassment. Friendship will always involve the risk of rejection, hurt, and being let down. It is in giving that we receive. It is in hazarding our lives for others that we find life and friendship. We are not to seek friends for ourselves, but to be friends to others. We are not to look to our own interests, but to those of Jesus and of others. This is where true joy is to be found. The definition of joy often used in Sunday school is J(esus) O(thers) Y(ou)—in that order. Epaphroditus had this order right, and that is why Paul expected him to bring joy (vs. 29). Paul tells us to honor people like that.

In Paul, Timothy, and Epaphroditus we see people who were following the example of Jesus Christ, who showed them and us the meaning of true friendship.

6 New Confidence

PHILIPPIANS 3:1-11

Finally, my brothers, rejoice in the Lord! It is no trouble for me to write the same things to you again, and it is a safeguard for you.
²Watch out for those dogs, those men who do evil, those mutilators of the flesh.
³For it is we who are the circumcision, we who worship by the Spirit of God, who glory in Christ Jesus, and who put no confidence in the flesh—⁴though I myself have reasons for such confidence.

If anyone else thinks he has reasons to put confidence in the flesh, I have more: ⁵circumcised on the eighth day, of the people of Israel, of the tribe of Benjamin, a Hebrew of Hebrews; in regard to the law, a Pharisee; as for zeal, persecuting the church; as for legalistic righteousness, faultless.

⁷But whatever was to my profit I now consider loss for the sake of Christ. ⁸What is more, I consider everything a loss compared to the surpassing greatness of knowing Christ Jesus my Lord, for whose sake I have lost all things. I consider them rubbish, that I may gain Christ ⁹and be found in him, not having a righteousness of my own that comes from the law, but that which is through faith in Christ—the righteousness that comes from God and is by faith. ¹⁰I want to know Christ and the power of his resurrection and the fellowship of sharing in his sufferings, becoming like him in his death, ¹¹and so, somehow, to attain to the resurrection from the dead.

Overconfidence can verge on arrogance. George Bernard Shaw said, "My speciality is being right when other people are wrong." Taken to the extreme, overconfidence can verge on blasphemy. King Alfonso X of Spain (1252-1284) said, "Had I been present at the creation, I would have given some useful hints for the better ordering of the universe."

The atheist philosopher Friedrich Nietzsche said, "There cannot be a God because, if there were one, I would not believe that I was not He." This kind of overconfidence is often based on academic prowess, power, money, success, or good looks (or mere stupidity!).

On the other hand are those who feel totally worthless. They are inwardly afraid, suffering from a sense of inadequacy and insecurity. Often those whom we would expect to be confident are, in fact, lacking in confidence. Christian psychologist James Dobson, in *Preparing for Adolescence,* points out that eighty percent of teenagers don't like the way they look, and often that feeling carries on beyond adolescence.[28] Those who are regarded as beautiful often lack confidence, even in their looks. The film star Michelle Pfeiffer said, "I've got small boobs, big lips, and a bent nose. My face is completely wrecked. I have never been confident about my looks." Another film star, Julia Roberts, said, "My mouth is too big and my smile is too gummy. Only my wardrobe people know how paranoid I am about my body. I say—'Let's get one thing straight: these are parts of me that I have a problem with, these are the ones we will hide. This is your job.'"

It is not just about looks; it may be that a lack of confidence goes much deeper. Madonna has said:

All of my will has always been to conquer some horrible feeling of inadequacy. I'm always struggling with that fear. I push past one spell of it and discover myself as a special human being and then I get to another stage and think I'm mediocre and uninteresting. And I find a way to get myself out of that. Again and again. My drive in life is from this horrible fear of being mediocre, and that's always pushing me, pushing me. Because even though I've become Somebody, I still have to prove that I'm *Somebody*. My struggle has never ended and it probably never will.[29]

Michael Jackson has described himself as "the world's loneliest man," saying that he still feels just as he did at school when "there was one girl I liked but I wasn't able to tell her. I was too embarrassed."

Should we be confident? If so, how can we be confident? What is true confidence? What is false confidence?

FALSE CONFIDENCE (VSS. 1-6)

True circumcision is circumcision of the heart, by the Spirit.

Paul warns the Philippian Christians to watch out for those whom he describes as filthy "dogs" (Philippians 3:2)—by which he means not household pets, but wild dogs that roam the streets, fighting and scavenging. He is referring to a group who have infiltrated the church and are insisting that the new Christians at Philippi should be circumcised, forcing a Jewish rite on Gentile Christians in order to make them "real Christians," arguing that faith in Jesus Christ is not enough. Paul describes them as "those men who do evil," in league with the "evil one," and "mutilators of the flesh." Paul derides their false confidence in circumcision.

It is true that Paul circumcised Timothy (Acts 16:3). But he did so for social reasons, so that he would be acceptable in Jewish homes (rather than as a condition for salvation). This group insisted on circumcision, not to make men acceptable to the Jews, but to make them acceptable to God. Paul insists that this is unnecessary. Christians are already circumcised (vs. 3), for in their hearts they are set apart for God. True circumcision is "circumcision of the heart, by the Spirit" (Romans 2:29). It is not the outward form that matters— just as it does not matter what form worship takes or where we worship. What matters is that we worship "by the Spirit of God" (vs. 3).

By insisting on circumcision, this group is suggesting that faith in Jesus Christ is not enough to be confident before God. They claim that confidence before God requires circumcision. However, true Christians "glory in Christ Jesus" (vs. 3) and in Him alone. They put "no confidence in the flesh." There is nothing that we can add to what Jesus achieved for us on the Cross.

If indeed there were other factors that could enhance one's standing before God, Paul declares he has many of them: "though I myself have reasons for such confidence. If anyone else thinks he has reasons to put confidence in the flesh, I have more" (vs. 4). He then lists several areas that might have given him confidence but which, in fact, only give a false confidence. The first four come by birth and the last three by voluntary choice.

Confidence from birth

Paul's first reason for confidence from his birth was that he had the outward marks of religion. He had been "circumcised on the eighth day" (vs. 5). His parents had not been heathens, but Jewish believers. As a baby he had received the outward marks of being a member of God's family. Although baptism is not the exact equivalent of circumcision, on its own it is not enough. Baptism is, among other things, the visible sign of entry into the church, but it is not enough to make us confident before God.

The second reason for Paul's confidence was his national

privilege. Paul says he is "of the people of Israel" (vs. 5). Many felt that being part of God's chosen people was a ground of security before God. Today there are those whose pride in their nationality gives them a false confidence before God. For some it is because they are Israeli, for others because they are British, or American, or some other nationality. It is almost as if they think that God could not refuse to accept "a true Brit" or an American or Canadian citizen.

The third possible basis for Paul's confidence was his family background, which was impeccable: "of the tribe of Benjamin" (vs. 5). Benjamin alone of the twelve patriarchs was born in the land of promise, and the tribe held the post of honor among the armies of the nation. The tribe of Benjamin gave to the Israelites their first King. Paul (previously known as Saul) probably derived his name directly or indirectly from King Saul, the Benjaminite.

Today many derive confidence from their background: their ancestry, their schooling, their class, or even their name. Others rely on "ecclesiastical heredity." They say, for example, "I am the child or grandchild of Christian parents," or "My great uncle was a bishop, therefore I must be acceptable to God." None of these things can give us confidence before God.

Many derive confidence from their background.

The fourth reason Paul might have had for confidence was his racial purity. Paul was "a Hebrew of Hebrews." Not only was Paul a Hebrew in the sense that both his parents were Hebrews, but he had the language and manners of a Hebrew. Apparently, he even spoke Hebrew at home, unlike many other Jews. He frequently quoted from the Hebrew Scriptures and retained the Hebrew culture.

Again, today there are those who pride themselves in their racial purity. They feel confident because of their language, their manners, and their etiquette. But these are not grounds of confidence before God.

Confidence from personal achievements

As well as being confident regarding his birth, Paul's achievements gave him further grounds for confidence.

First he had been religious. He was "in regard to the law, a Pharisee" (vs. 5). Paul belonged to the strictest sect in Judaism and was scrupulous in keeping every law and every rule. He believed in God, he prayed, and he gave money. There are some today who say, "I have never done anyone any harm," or "I have never been in trouble with the law," or "I have always been very religious." But none of these things can give us confidence before God.

Second, Paul had been utterly sincere in his beliefs and energetic in carrying out what he believed to be God's will, that is, "persecuting the church" (vs. 6). No one could question his zeal.

Sincerity of belief is not enough. Some say, "It doesn't matter what you believe so long as you are sincere." But it is possible to be sincerely wrong. Paul had been sincerely wrong in persecuting the Christian church.

The third achievement Paul had previously regarded as a reason for confidence was the fact that he had led a good life. As far as "legalistic righteousness" was concerned, Paul was "faultless" (vs. 6). In the days before his conversion Paul was not burdened with a bad conscience or torn apart by inner conflict. He regard-

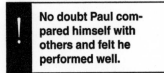

No doubt Paul compared himself with others and felt he performed well.

ed himself as without fault. No doubt he compared himself with others and felt he performed well.

Today there are many who have great problems with the idea that they need forgiveness. They feel they have led a good life and that they have reasons for confidence before God.

I play quite a lot of squash. By comparison with a beginner, my game is not too bad. Not long ago I watched Chris Dittmar (who was then the world's number two squash player) playing on the court opposite me. Soon I realized that I had not even begun to play good squash. By analogy, as people look around at others, they feel that they are not doing too badly. When we look at Jesus, we realize we have hardly even begun.

Indeed none of the achievements of the secular world can bring true confidence, no matter what we achieve in terms of career, success, academic achievement, fame, money, or importance.

As Paul's "accountant's eye travels down the list"[30] he adds up all the things that gave him confidence before. He used to regard them as "profit" (vs. 7). Now, as he does his sums, the bottom line is a heavy "loss" (vs. 7). He rejects all those things with disgust. He describes them as "rubbish" (vs. 8). The word means either waste foods consigned to the garbage heap, or human excrement.

All the things that brought Paul confidence before he was a Christian, he now regards as useless when contrasted with something immeasurably greater. Now he has a totally new confidence.

TRUE CONFIDENCE (VSS. 7-9)

All the things that gave Paul confidence in the past and that he regarded as profit, he now considers as "loss compared to the surpassing greatness of knowing Christ Jesus" (vs. 8). This is where his new confidence comes from. One day Paul encountered Jesus Christ. From that day onward he lived in a vital, lively, continuing relationship with Jesus Christ.

It is possible to know Jesus, the man whom we read about in the pages of the New Testament. We do not see Him physically, but we can talk to Him and listen to Him speaking to us. We can spend time in His presence, we can experience His love, and we can know Him as Paul knew Him.

Often we hear people name-dropping. They are so proud that they know someone rich or famous; it bolsters their confidence. But that is nothing compared to knowing the King of kings and Lord of lords, and speaking to Him in an intimate way each day. No wonder Paul had a completely new confidence.

This new relationship stemmed from a new righteousness. Paul considers all his previous qualifications as "rubbish, that I may gain

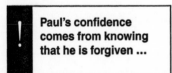

Paul's confidence comes from knowing that he is forgiven ...

Christ and be found in him, not having a righteousness of my own that comes from the law, but that which is through faith in Christ— the righteousness that comes from God and is by faith" (vss. 8, 9). Paul had found another righteousness, quite unlike his previous self-righteousness. Now he sees that he does not have a righteousness of his own: "No one will be declared righteous in his sight by observing the law; rather, through the law we become conscious of sin" (Romans 3:20).

To be righteous before God means, in the words of Professor

Gordon Fee, "to have a right relationship with a righteous God demonstrated in right living that reflects the character of God." This cannot be achieved on our own, but only received as a gift from God (vs. 9). We do not deserve it and we cannot earn it. Jesus made it possible by what He did on the cross (Romans 3:21-26). As Calvin said, "The Son of God, utterly clean of all fault, nevertheless took upon himself the shame and reproach of our iniquities, and in return clothed us with his purity."[31] This great exchange that took place on the cross gives us supreme confidence. We have confidence about the past for we know that we are totally forgiven. We are "justified not only from the sins committed before the time of belief," but "from *all* guilt."[32]

We, like Paul, have confidence about the future. Paul had encountered the risen Jesus and he therefore knew that one day he too would rise. Professor Gordon Fee explains, "The resurrection of Jesus

has already set the future in motion. It makes our resurrection inevitable. The resurrection of Jesus was the first fruits that guarantees the final harvest." Not only do we know that we too will be resurrected, but we can have confidence on the Day of Judgment.

So, the entire length and breadth of our life is made secure in

Christ. We can have confidence in the present also as we receive God's righteousness, not by doing anything, but "through faith in Christ" (vs. 9), or "by faith," as Paul puts it at the end of the verse. Faith is not a way of earning the gift; rather it is the way in which we receive the gift. If someone gives us a present, we cannot say we earned it. However, we do have to receive it, unwrap it, and enjoy it. By faith we receive and enjoy God's gift.

This is what gave Paul confidence before God and boldness before men so that he could say, "We are always confident" (2 Corinthians 5:6). His confidence comes from knowing that he is forgiven and that God sees him as righteous through Christ. He has access to the presence of God. As he said elsewhere, "In him and through faith in him we may approach God with freedom and confidence" (Ephesians 3:12). Here we see the great difference between false and true confidence. "Secular self-esteem involves valuing oneself over and against God. Christian self-esteem involves valuing oneself in and through Christ."[33]

Martin Luther (1483-1546) was at one time a budding lawyer who tried to live a righteous life. Much to his father's disappointment, he became a monk. He fasted for days, spent sleepless nights in prayer, and beat himself to get free of his bodily desires. Yet he was still plagued by how one could stand in holiness before a righteous and demanding God. Then one day, as he read his New Testament, he understood what Paul meant by the righteousness of God. He wrote afterwards:

> I had indeed been captivated with an extraordinary ardor for understanding Paul in the epistle to the Romans ... But a single word in Chapter 1:17 "in it the righteousness of God is revealed" ... had stood in my way. For I hated that word "righteousness of God"... I had been taught to understand [that] God is righteous and punishes the unrighteous sinner.
>
> I raged with a fierce and troubled conscience ... [until] I

began to understand that the righteousness of God is that by which the righteous lives by a gift of God, namely by faith ... here I felt that I was altogether born again and had entered paradise itself through open gates. There a totally other face of the entire Scripture showed itself to me ...

And I extolled my sweetest word with a love as great as the hatred with which I had before hated the word "righteousness of God." Thus that place in Paul was for me truly the gate to paradise.[34]

This insight that God justifies us by faith is our objective ground of confidence before God and boldness before other people.

In practice, this confidence may take time to grow. William Pitt, Earl of Chatham (1708-1778), said in a different context, "Confidence is a plant of slow growth." The person whose life is centered on Jesus Christ can go through life with a growing confidence. Our confidence and self-esteem will grow as we realize what is already ours in Christ. The best environment for this plant to grow is in the community of the Christian church, if it is a loving, encouraging, and affirming environment.

7 New Ambitions

PHILIPPIANS 3:10-21

[10]I want to know Christ and the power of his resurrection and the fellowship of sharing in his sufferings, becoming like him in his death, [11]and so, somehow, to attain to the resurrection from the dead.

[12]Not that I have already obtained all this, or have already been made perfect, but I press on to take hold of that for which Christ Jesus took hold of me. [13]Brothers, I do not consider myself yet to have taken hold of it. But one thing I do: Forgetting what is behind and straining toward what is ahead, [14]I press on toward the goal to win the prize for which God has called me heavenward in Christ Jesus.

[15]All of us who are mature should take such a view of things. And if on some point you think differently, that too God will make clear to you. [16]Only let us live up to what we have already attained.

[17]Join with others in following my example, brothers, and take note of those who live according to the pattern we gave you. [18]For, as I have often told you before and now say again even with tears, many live as enemies of the cross of Christ. [19]Their destiny is destruction, their god is their stomach, and their glory is in their shame. Their mind is on earthly things. [20]But our citizenship is in heaven. And we eagerly await a Savior from there, the Lord Jesus Christ, [21]who, by the power that enables him to bring everything under his control, will transform our lowly bodies so that they will like his glorious body.

Should a Christian be ambitious? Some cannot see the problem. They go to church on Sunday and during the rest of the week they pursue their own ambitions. Others think that when you become a Christian you have to give up all ambitions and simply drift through life taking whatever comes as "God's will." They see all ambition as sin, much like Shakespeare's Henry VIII does in his appeal to Thomas Cromwell: "Cromwell, I charge thee, fling away ambition: By that sin fell the angels . . . "

By contrast, Paul was fiercely ambitious. Ambition has been defined as the "desire to succeed." Before he was a Christian, Paul had been fiercely ambitious in his desire to persecute the church. After his conversion he did not lose his ambitious nature, but its direction changed. If anything, he was even more ambitious! He describes himself  in Philippians 3:10-20 as being like an athlete desperate to win a race.

But what is Paul's ambition? John Stott makes the point that "ultimately there are only two controlling ambitions . . . our own glory, and the other, God's."[35]

GOD'S GLORY—JESUS-CENTERED AMBITION (VSS. 10-17)

We saw in the last chapter that Paul's confidence came from knowing Christ and having His righteousness. Mid-sentence, he moves from the ground of his confidence to the focus of his ambitions. First, his ambition is "to know Christ" (vs. 10). The Greek word for "to know" means far more than intellectual knowledge, but includes personal knowledge. Paul's ambition is not just to know about Christ, but to know Him as a person. The word used is the same as that used in the Greek translation of the Hebrew word in Genesis when the writer says that "Adam knew Eve his wife; and she conceived and bore Cain" (Genesis 4:1, *Revised Standard Version*). Paul's ambition is to know Christ in an exhilarating and intimate union. This is the new focus of his life.

The power of His resurrection

Paul goes on to elaborate what he means by this intimate relationship with Christ. Second, it means to know "the power of his resurrection" (vs. 10), not just as a past event in history, but as a dynamic power at work in his life. Paul says elsewhere that "if the Spirit of him who raised Jesus from the dead is living in you, he who raised Christ from the dead will also give life to your mortal bodies through his Spirit, who lives in you" (Romans 8:11). The Spirit of God brings this resurrection power to our lives. By the power of His death and resurrection, Jesus disarmed Satan, broke the hold of sin, and defeated death. This power is available to all to enable us to live holy lives and minister to others with the resurrection power. Paul's ambition is to know that power more and more.

Sharing in His sufferings

Third, for Paul, knowing Christ involves "the fellowship of sharing in his sufferings, becoming like him in his death" (vs. 10). He does not seek suffering, but he sees it as inevitable. It is not a penalty but a privilege. The suffering and death of Jesus are different from ours in that He died for our sins to save us from what we deserve. We will never suffer in exactly the way He did. Rather, our sufferings are the practical results of our Christian life. For some, this will mean severe persecution as it did for Paul and millions of Christians around the world today. For all of us, it involves following "the downward path of the Crucified"[36] and it will include "all the pangs and afflictions undergone in the struggle against sin either within or without."[37] It is at these moments of suffering that we experience fellowship with Christ, and it is that fellowship Paul wants—whatever the cost.

On April 20, 1999, two students went on a rampage at Columbine High School in Littleton, Colorado, murdering 13 people and injuring many others. Several of those targeted were Christians.

Among them was 17-year-old Cassie Bernall. Just a few years earlier, she had dabbled in the occult, including witchcraft. She had embraced the same darkness and nihilism that drove her killers to such despicable acts. But two years before, Cassie gave her life to Christ, and she was transformed. One of her friends described her as "a light for Christ." Cassie was known for carrying a Bible to school, the same Bible she was reading when the two young killers burst into the school library. One of the masked gunmen pointed his weapon at her and asked, "Do you believe in God?"

Cassie knew that if she said "yes" she would pay with her life. She paused and then answered, "Yes, I believe in God."

"Why?" asked the gunman, but she had no chance to respond, for he had already shot her dead.

Sharing His destiny

Fourth, knowing Christ means sharing His destiny, "somehow, to attain to the resurrection from the dead" (vs. 11). When Paul says "somehow," he is expressing humility, not doubt. Paul never doubted that one day we would go to be with Christ (Philippians 1:20-23; 3:20, 21). His future hope does not depend on himself but on what Christ has done for him on the Cross. Yet he is not arrogant about this hope; he is not there yet. He sees this as a future event, as opposed to those who were saying that the Resurrection had already happened and that they were already perfect. Paul says that he is not there yet, but it is his aim and ambition (vss. 12 and following).

Paul is single-minded about his ambition—"one thing I do" (vs. 13). This does not mean he neglected other areas of his life. Rather, it means that all else was subordinated to his overriding ambition. Ignatius of Loyola (1491-1556), founder of the Jesuits, wrote:

Human persons are created to praise, reverence and serve God ... The other things on the face of the earth are created for us, to

84

help us in attaining the purpose for which we are created. Therefore, we are to make use of them insofar as they help us to attain our purpose, and we should rid ourselves of them insofar as they hinder us from attaining it.

It is not wrong to have ambitions for marriage, family life, career, work, and ministry. Indeed, it is entirely appropriate that we should; but all such ambitions must be subordinated to our ambition to know Christ. He is our first priority in life and nothing in our life should conflict with that ambition.

Chuck Colson was a self-made man. As a student, he turned down a scholarship to Harvard in an arrogant manner. Later he joined the Marines, set up his own law firm, and entered politics. By the age of forty, he had become one of President Nixon's closest confidants. Later he described himself as "a young ambitious political king maker ... [like Nixon] of ... lower middle-class origins, men who'd known hard work all our lives, prideful men seeking that most elusive goal of all—acceptance and the respect of those who had spurned us in earlier years." Branded by a *Wall Street Journal* headline as "*Nixon hatchet-man call it what you will, Chuck Colson handles President's dirty work*," he became a Christian, partly as a result of reading C. S. Lewis' *Mere Christianity*. He pleaded guilty to his part in the Watergate cover-up and was sentenced to one to three years' imprisonment.

When Colson left the court after sentencing he said, "What happened in court today . . . was the court's will and the Lord's will—I have committed my life to Jesus Christ and I can work for Him in prison as well as out."[38] And he did. After his release, Colson set up Prison Christian Fellowship and has been directly or indirectly responsible for leading thousands to Christ. I once heard him say on the radio, "I was ambitious, and I am ambitious today, but I hope it is not for Chuck Colson (though I struggle quite a lot, as a matter of fact). But I am ambitious for Christ."

Paul was a man who was ambitious for Christ, although no doubt he too struggled with it at times. He sees himself as an athlete for Christ, racing in a stadium. Like a runner, the Christian must not look back—"forgetting what is behind" (vs. 13). We cannot live on past successes or rest on former laurels. Nor should we be bogged down by past failures, despair over past sins, or bitterness over past wrongs done to us. We are not to dwell on the past.

Continuing with the image of the racer, Paul says, "Straining towards what is ahead, I press on towards the goal to win the prize for which God has called me heavenwards in Christ Jesus" (vss. 13, 14). It is a picture of an athlete stretching out, straining every muscle as he goes all out for the finish. Paul brings to mind the striking image of Eric Liddell, the Olympic runner whose story was retold in the film *Chariots of Fire*, chest out, head held high, legs and arms pumping furiously as he tore down the back straight to the finish to win the gold medal. It is with the same determination that Paul pursues his ambition to know Christ. Paul urges the Christians at Philippi to follow his example. He should not be alone in his aims and ambitions: "All of us who are mature should take such a view of things. And if on some point you think differently, that too God will make clear to you. Only let us live up to what we have already attained" (vss. 15, 16). Indeed, he is not alone. Already others have followed his example, and he encourages them to do the same: "Join with others in following my example, brothers, and take note of those who live according to the pattern we gave you" (vs. 17).

OUR GLORY—SELF-CENTERED AMBITION (VSS. 17-21)

Paul was a tough man. He had been flogged and tortured, but he did not cry tears of physical pain; rather, he sang hymns of praise. He had troubles, hardships, and distresses; he had been through beatings, imprisonment, and riots; he had faced sleepless nights and hunger (2 Corinthians 6:4-7). None of this reduced him to tears of anguish and despair. Yet now he shed tears, not of self-pity, but of sadness about the "many [who] live as enemies of the cross of Christ" (vs. 18). In rejecting the forgiveness and freedom that Christ died to bring, consciously or unconsciously, they are effectively rejecting Him and His achievement on the Cross. Paul sees that they are missing out on "the resurrection of the dead," and their terrible end is "destruction" (vs. 19). No doubt they are unaware of where they are heading. The devil never tells us our destination as he leads us along his path, but Paul sees that "their destiny is destruction" (vs. 19).

Who are these people and why are they heading for destruction? Paul tells us three things about them, which show us that their ambitions were in an entirely different direction to those of Paul. They were man-centered ambitions.

Their appetites dictate their lifestyle

First, their appetites dictate their lifestyle. Paul tells us that "their god is their stomach" (vs. 19). For some, their lives literally revolve around their eating and drinking habits. But we need not interpret it quite so narrowly. Surely Paul is referring to those whose god is personal satisfaction and whose lives revolve around sensuality.

Of course, God made us sensual beings. Jesus Himself became flesh (John 1:14). The body is not evil. We were created to enjoy all our bodily senses—whether sight, smell, hearing, touch, or taste. There is nothing wrong with enjoying food, music, exercise, clothes, or sexual pleasure within the limits God has prescribed. What is wrong is when these things become our god and displace the one true God, Jesus Christ, at the center of our lives.

Sadly, it is as true today as it was in Paul's day that much of our world revolves around sensuality. One only has to look at popular magazines. In one magazine I came across recently, virtually every page was devoted to sex, food, clothing, exercise, drink, perfume, and jewelry. It was all about the body: how to clothe it, exercise it, feed it, decorate it, and make it smell good. Sensual pleasure dominated virtually every page. Shoes were advertised like this: "Slip into something more comfortable. Feel the lycra caress every contour of your skin, as you float along … go on, show your feet you love them, give them a hug." Skin cream was advertised thus: "With its millions of droplets, even smaller than liposomes, the microcrystal textures as thin as muslin enticing and amazing, will make you experience new sensations." A vacation spa promoted itself as "the body holiday"—"Give us your body for a week and we will give you back your mind. It is all your body could ask for." Many of the advertisements suggested that their products had a god-like quality; so the vodka was described as "absolute perfection," the perfume was called "Eternity," and the ice cream was "dedicated to pleasure."

Many people's lives revolve directly or indirectly around satisfying their bodily desires. For some it is as direct as in the advertisements. For others the direct ambition is money or power or ambition. Such ambitions always lead to dissatisfaction. The same magazine with all the advertisements carried an article about Mick Jagger, who is over fifty and a grandfather. Two years before, he had completed the most successful world tour in the Rolling Stones' history, grossing $120 million. He is in the top hundred of Britain's richest people—one of the wealthiest members of the rock elite. He has four houses in Britain and the United States worth over $12 million. He is a friend of the rich, titled, famous, and even royalty. He has five children by three different women. His girlfriends have included some of the most beautiful women in the world. He has fame, money, and influence. Yet his friend Keith Richards says, "99% of the male population of the Western world—and beyond—would give a limb to live the life of Jagger, to be Mick Jagger ... and he's not happy being Mick Jagger." The article ends by saying that "nearly 30 years after the Stones' most defining moment in song, the one certain thing about Mick is that he is unsatisfied still."

Much of our world revolves around sensuality.

They boast when they should blush

The second thing Paul tells us about "the enemies of the cross" is that they boast when they should blush. He writes: "Their glory is in their shame" (vs. 19). They are like robbers who boast about their ill-gotten gains, or those who have stored up treasures for themselves and show you around their estate with great pride, or those who boast of their sexual conquests or how much they drank the night before. They have achieved their ambitions and glory in them, but these gods are false.

Their minds are locked into this planet

Third, their minds are locked into this planet. Paul says: "Their mind is on earthly things" (vs. 19). Jesus said: "Where your treasure is, there your heart will be also" (Matthew 6:21). If our ambitions are sensual, our thoughts will be earthly. If our ambition is to know Christ, our hearts will soar into the heavenly places.

The Christian is a citizen of heaven. Paul returns once again to the familiar image of citizenship. In Philippians 1:27 he had urged the Philippians to be worthy citizens of heaven. He reminds them of their true home, where their hearts should be set. The great desire of every colony was to invite the Roman emperor to visit. From 48 A.D. he was given the title "Savior of Mankind." As Philippi awaited a worldly savior, so Christians await a heavenly Savior.

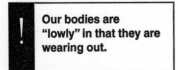

The emperor would bring gifts or relief from taxes. The Lord Jesus Christ, "by the power that enables him to bring everything under his control, will transform our lowly bodies so that they will be like his glorious body" (vs. 21). Our bodies are "lowly" in that they are wearing out. Our bodily strength gradually fails, our mental powers wane. Our eyesight fails, we experience humiliating illness. Our bodies are also lowly in that we constantly need to battle against temptation in order to control our tongues and our appetites. Hence, it is absurd to make a god out of them. The irony is that if we make our bodies our god, our destiny must logically be destruction. We all die. If we seek God's glory, then Jesus will transform these bodies, which are subject to decay and sin, to be like "his glorious body," which will never age or decay and will not be subject to sinful desires.

> **!** Our bodies are "lowly" in that they are wearing out.

It is the certainty of our own bodily resurrection and the promise of eternity with God that motivates us to "press on to take hold of that for which Christ Jesus took hold of me." As we look to Jesus Christ on the cross, we see God's love for us—which then transforms our life and informs our vision and purpose for our own time here on earth.

In 1865, slavery was abolished in the United States, but it was replaced by segregation—laws and practices that excluded black people from the rest of society. For example, in Montgomery, Alabama, the first ten seats of every bus were reserved for white people. Black people sitting anywhere else in the bus were expected to give up their seat to a white person when these rows were full.

Rosa Parks, a 42-year-old tailor's assistant in a Montgomery department store, was travelling home on the bus after a hard day's work on December 1, 1955. She was sitting in the eleventh row.

Six white people got on and the bus driver called to her: "You! You get up." She refused, commenting later, "I knew someone had to take the first step and I made up my mind not to move."

The bus driver called the police and she was arrested and imprisoned. Looking back, she observed that she had always been a timid person, but "my entire life has demanded of me that I be courageous."

This spontaneous individual action by the Christian woman gave rise to a collective movement that would force the U.S. to confront its legacy of racial inequality. In the words of one black leader, "At that moment, somewhere in the universe, a gear in the machinery shifted."

On Monday, December 5, the boycott of the buses began. Thousands gathered that night to hear Martin Luther King preach at Holt Street Baptist Church. Unsurprisingly, he spoke of Rosa Parks, saying, "Nobody can doubt the height of her character. No one can doubt the depth of her Christian commitment and devotion to the teaching of Jesus Christ. And, you know friends, there comes a time when people get tired of being trampled over by the iron feet of oppression."

But those iron feet of oppression deprived both Rosa and her husband of their jobs in the following weeks, and threats were made to kill them. But Rosa Parks was not easily frightened by death, observing, "Well, you have to die sometime. If this boycott happens to be attributed to me and my actions and they killed me, then I would just be dead."

On November 13, 1959, the Supreme Court ruled that the Montgomery Segregated Seating Ordinance was unconstitutional. This led to a bombing campaign in which several black churches and homes of ministers were destroyed. On Friday, December 21, 1956, integrated bus service began in Montgomery.

In 1980, Rosa Parks became the first woman to receive the martin Luther King non-violent peace prize. The same year, *Ebony Magazine* honored her as the living black woman who had done the most to advance the cause of civil rights. In 1984, at the age of 71, she demonstrated against the racial policies of the South African government.

Years before, when she had defied segregation, she had vowed, "I plan not to give up until all are free. We are all soldiers and we must keep on as long as we can in this battle for freedom and justice for all."

Rosa Parks was following the path of Paul, the path of Chuck Colson, the path of Cassie Bernall: "The downward path of the crucified."

In this passage Paul tells us that everyone is on one of two paths. There are two destinations: one is heading for heaven, the resurrection of the dead, and the transformation of our bodies to be like "his glorious body." The other is heading for destruction (vs. 19). There are two powers at work: the resurrection power of the Holy Spirit (vs. 10) and the power of bodily appetites (vs. 19). There are two possible lifestyles: those willing to share in His sufferings, and those who want a lifestyle of ease and comfort. There are two possible gods: our Lord Jesus Christ, or our "stomachs." There are two possible attitudes to Jesus: either friendship at an intimate level, or enemies of the Cross. Ultimately, there are only two possible ambitions: either His glory (Philippians 3:3), Jesus-centered ambition; or our own glory, self-centered ambition. Paul says, in effect: "I have changed my ambitions. Now I am Jesus-centered. Will you join me?"

8 New Resources

PHILIPPIANS 4:1-9

Therefore, my brothers, you whom I love and long for, my joy and my crown, that is how you should stand firm in the Lord, dear friends!

²I plead with Euodia and I plead with Syntyche to agree with each other in the Lord. ³Yes, and I ask you, loyal yokefellow, help these women who have contended at my side in the cause of the gospel, along with Clement and the rest of my fellow workers, whose names are in the book life.

⁴Rejoice in the Lord always. I will say it again: Rejoice! ⁵Let your gentleness be evident to all. The Lord is near. ⁶Do not be anxious about anything, but in everything, by prayer and petition, with thanksgiving, present your requests to God. ⁷And the peace of God, which transcends all understanding, will guard your hearts and your minds in Christ Jesus.

⁸Finally, brothers, whatever is true, whatever is noble, whatever is right, whatever is pure, whatever is lovely, whatever is admirable—if anything is excellent or praiseworthy—think about such things. ⁹Whatever you have learned or received or heard from me, or seen in me—put it into practice. And the God of peace will be with you.

On March 2, 1975, I heard a talk by the Reverend E.J.H. Nash, a very wise seventy-six-year-old, who had spent most of his life involved in the pastoral care of young Christians and who had a major impact on my own life. The subject was, "Where will you be in ten years' time?" I was only nineteen at the time, and ten years seemed like an eternity, but the title of the talk struck me with such force that I have never forgotten it. Rev. Nash made me realize the importance of laying firm foundations as early as possible in order to avoid being side-tracked.

In a similar vein, the apostle Paul writes to the Christians at Philippi with advice on how they can "stand firm" in the Lord (Philippians 4:1). The word used is the same as that for a soldier standing fast in the shock of battle with the enemy surging down upon him, or a combatant in a Roman amphitheater fighting for his life. In the same way, "the believers are condemned to fight for their lives: against them are arrayed the ranks of worldliness and sin: only unflinching courage and steady combination can win the victory against such odds."[40] Paul tells the Philippians in this passage how they can not only hold off the enemy but come through victorious, full of joy, peace, and a sense of the presence of God.

Paul writes to a group of people he regards as "dear friends" (vs. 1). More than that, they are "brothers" whom he loves and longs for. They are his "joy and crown" (vs. 1). The word for "crown" does not imply dominion; rather, it carries the idea of victory and merriment.

It is a word used for the crown or wreath given to a victorious athlete at the Greek games. To win the crown was the peak of the

athlete's ambition. The same word was used for the crown with which a guest was adorned at a banquet—a time of great joy. Such is Paul's feeling about the Christians at Philippi. He led them to the Lord and watched them grow as Christians. Now they bring him great joy, and he wants to ensure that they will not fall away. So he passes on to them some of the secrets of standing firm in the Lord.

WATCH YOUR RELATIONSHIPS WITH OTHER CHRISTIANS (VSS. 2, 3)

We saw earlier (Chapter 2) how Paul likened the Christians at Philippi to a Greek phalanx standing shoulder to shoulder. They were virtually invincible, provided they did not break rank. The enemy is always looking for cracks and divisions in the church, which he can so easily exploit. One of the most common causes of division and splits in the church is personality clashes.

Here we see an example of a personality clash, which Paul abhors. Two women, Euodia and Syntyche, possibly business friends of Lydia, have fallen out with each other. They appear to have been leaders of the church, since Paul knows their names, and they have taken an active part with Paul as fellow workers, possibly as leaders of house congregations.

Paul does not take sides (which suggests it was not a doctrinal dispute); rather, he urges both of them to take the initiative in order to reach agreement, and he appeals to others to help bring them together. He does not criticize them; rather, he concentrates on their good points to build them up—they have contended by his side and their "names are in the book of life" (vs. 3).

Paul is aware that even trivial personality clashes like this can lead people away from the Lord. A few years ago, I went to stay with a highly intelligent couple in Liverpool. I discovered that they had both been Christians when they married. However, after seven years of marriage, the wife had fallen away from the Lord. For fifteen years, this woman refused to go to church and argued strongly against the Christian faith. Eventually I discovered the event that had caused her to give up her faith.

Even trivial personality clashes can lead people away from the Lord.

She had been to the church fête. She went to the cake stall and bought a cake. Seeing another cake she wanted she said, "I'll have that one as well." The woman behind the stall said, "Oh, no, you can't have two." She was deeply offended by the unfriendliness, felt that the church was full of hypocrites, and never went back. About six months after I stayed with them, they moved to a new house. Because the new house was near a different church, she attended a service. She later said that the moment she walked into the church it was "like coming home." She came back to the Lord and asked Him to heal her of a serious medical condition—Depuytren's contracture—for which she would have to have an operation. God healed her miraculously. Later she wrote to me and said, "It is lovely to know that God wants me in His family after all I said against Him!"

God's love is indeed remarkable, but it was sad that she had wasted fifteen years of Christian service because of a personality clash. We need to watch carefully our relationships with other Christians. While disagreements, disunity, and unforgiveness can weaken the church and destroy our faith, the warmth of close Christian friendships strengthens the church, builds our faith, and is one of the vital secrets of standing firm in the Lord.

WATCH YOUR RELATIONSHIP WITH THE LORD (VSS. 4-7)

Obviously the key to standing firm "in the Lord" is our relationship with Him. How can we ensure that we stay close to Him? Paul gives us three invaluable tips.

Enjoy the Lord (vs. 4)

Sixteen times Paul urges the Christians at Philippi to rejoice. Here he says it twice: "Rejoice in the Lord always. I will say it again: Rejoice!" (vs. 4).

Paul never denies the problems, but he does encourage the Philippians to rejoice in the midst of difficulties.

It is said that "the optimist sees the doughnut, the pessimist sees the hole." There is something to be said for Christian optimism. But that is not what Paul is speaking about here. However bad our circumstances might be, there is one thing we can always rejoice about: the Lord, His love, His mercy, His promises, and His presence. On the other hand, however good our circumstances are, our chief ground of rejoicing should not be those, but the Lord. It is right to rejoice in a happy marriage, happy families, fulfilling jobs, fruitful ministries, and all the blessings of life, but Paul says our supreme ground for rejoicing should not be these things but the Lord, in whom true joy is to be found. If the joy of the Lord is our strength, then nothing can take that away, and we will have a solid anchor in our spiritual lives.

Expect the Lord (vs. 5)

"The Lord is near" (vs. 5). This is a reason for forbearance. Paul says, "Let your gentleness be evident to all" (vs. 5). The word for gentleness means "moderation" or "graciousness." It is the opposite of contention, abrasiveness, and self-seeking desires. It means being willing to forego retaliation. There is no need to defend ourselves, because the Lord is coming, and He will vindicate us.

The expression, "The Lord is near" probably has a deliberate double meaning. First, the Lord is near in time. We should expect Him at any moment. There is always great excitement when a famous person is expected to arrive. The crowds gather when a member of the royal family or a famous entertainer or politician is about to appear. What excitement there is at the thought that Jesus is about to come and we will see Him!

Second, the Lord is near in the sense that He is already present by His Spirit. We sense His presence, we speak to Him, we hear His voice in our hearts. We can't see Him, but we see all the signs of His presence. Abiding in His presence is one of the keys to standing firm in the Lord.

Entreat the Lord (vss. 6, 7)

Sir Winston Churchill said, "When I look back on all these worries I remember the story of the old man who said on his death bed that he had had a lot of trouble in his life, most of which never happened." Worry can wreck our lives. Dale Carnegie once wrote a book called *How to Stop Worrying and Start Living*. A life weighed down by worry is not really living.

Prayer and worry are not easy bedfellows. They are like fire and water. A sign outside a church reads: "Why pray when you can worry and take tranquilizers?" Paul says, "Do not be anxious about anything, but in everything, by prayer and petition, with thanksgiving, present your requests to God. And the peace of God, which transcends all understanding, will guard your hearts and your minds in Christ Jesus" (vss. 6, 7).

Paul urges us to pray in every situation: "in everything," when things are going well and when things are difficult. We need to be specific: "by prayer and petition ... present your requests to God" (vs. 6). Many people find it a help to keep a journal or prayer diary to write down specific requests. This not only aids concentration, but it also enables us to look back and see the ways in which God has answered our prayers. We can then pray "with thanksgiving" (vs. 6). As we give thanks, recollecting answered prayer, it increases our confidence in praying further.

The extraordinary and wonderful promise is that as we do this "the peace of God, which transcends all understanding, will guard your hearts and your minds in Christ Jesus" (vs. 7). Time and again, this has proved true in Christian experience. As we bring our worries and anxieties to God in prayer and leave them with Him, He gives us His peace in exchange. The word for peace means far more than an absence of hostility. It means wholeness, soundness, well-being, oneness with God, every kind of blessing and good. It is a peace "which transcends all understanding" in that it surpasses all our hopes and expectations. It transcends the understanding of others in that they cannot understand how we can be so peaceful when going through major worries and anxieties. Indeed, our minds can scarcely comprehend it either.

> **As we bring our anxieties to God, He gives us His peace in exchange.**

The "peace of God" keeps us close to the Lord. Paul says it will "guard your hearts and your minds in Christ Jesus." The word for "guard" is a military word used for standing on guard at the city gates. The peace of God protects us from the attacks that lead us away from the Lord, and it keeps us united with Him in heart and mind.

WATCH YOUR UNSEEN THOUGHTS (VS. 8)

What we think is more important than who we are and what we have. As has been said, "A man is not what he thinks he is, but what he thinks, he is." Jesus said that what goes into our mouths is not important, because that goes into our stomachs and then eventually leaves the body. What matters is what comes out of our mouths, because that comes from the heart and "out of the heart come evil thoughts, murder, adultery, sexual immorality, theft, false testimony, slander. These are what make a man 'unclean'" (Matthew 15:19, 20).

What we think will affect every area of our lives. There is a saying: "Sow a thought, reap an action, sow an action, reap a habit, sow a habit, reap a character, sow a character, reap a destiny." Knowing the importance of our thoughts, Paul urges us to set our minds on the right things; on things that are "true" as opposed to lies and falsehood; on "whatever is noble," things that are morally good; on what is "right" and just; on the things that are "pure" in terms of our motivation; on things that are "lovely" and attractive; on things that are "admirable" in the sense that they have a high tone and are of good repute. He summarizes the list by saying, "If anything is excellent or praiseworthy—think about such things" (vs. 8).

The way to get wrong thoughts out is to get right thoughts in.

It is hard to think like that, because the world we live in is quite different. We are surrounded by images and words from television, newspapers, films, advertising, conversation, and events that can so easily lead us in a different direction. Since Satan has access to our minds, we are bound to be tempted almost daily by wrong thoughts. However, as Martin Luther said, you can't stop a bird flying overhead, but you can stop it nesting in your hair.

The way to get wrong thoughts out is to get right thoughts in. Sir Thomas More said, "Occupy your minds with good thoughts, or the enemy will fill them with bad ones: unoccupied they cannot be." This, indeed, is Paul's solution.

How then, in practice, can we learn to think like this? We need to fill our minds with good thoughts from the moment we wake up. There is no better way of doing this than by beginning the day with Bible reading, worship, and prayer—to set the agenda right for the day. Memorizing Bible verses and reading Christian books can help to focus our minds on the right things. Many find it helpful to listen to tapes of worship, Bible reading, or Christian teaching in the car or when they are doing practical work. Whenever we can, it is good to

expose ourselves to the splendor of the natural world, to beautiful art, and anything else that falls into the categories Paul lists.

What we think about is not something that can be seen by others. It is part of our secret life with God, but it is vital to standing fast in the Lord. Our unseen life is like the roots of a tree or the foundation of a house, and our ability to withstand the storms of life depends on the strength of the unseen parts.

WATCH THE EXAMPLE OF OTHER CHRISTIANS (VS. 9)

Paul is not ashamed to put himself forward as an example of a life to be followed. He says, "Whatever you have learned or received or heard from me, or seen in me—put it into practice"(vs. 9). The word for "received" is a technical term used for receiving an authoritative tradition handed down from church leaders (1 Corinthians 11:23; 15:3). Of course, what we teach does not have the same authority as Paul's teaching, but our equivalent is the biblical teaching we pass on to others.

Paul encourages the Philippians not only to follow his teaching, but also his lifestyle, both his words and his actions: what they have heard and seen. It is not wrong to model our lives on those of other Christians whom we respect and admire. Indeed, it is often helpful to do so, provided that we model our lives on the right people— those who are modeling themselves on Jesus. The writer of Hebrews puts before his readers the example of the great men and women of God (Hebrews 11), but he goes on to urge his readers to fix their eyes on Jesus (Hebrews 12:2).

I mentioned earlier the time I saw one of the world's leading players, Chris Dittmar, playing squash. A friend and I watched him playing against another world-ranked player. After this, my friend and I played each other and we both played better than ever before! We were inspired by the match we had watched. In a far more wonderful way we are inspired as we look at the example of Jesus and as we look to the lives of others—those great men and women of God both past and present. I love to read the biographies of such people.

I have found in my own life that the lives of Christian friends have been a great influence on me. In some cases it has been their family life that has been the model; in others their prayer life, their love, their way of handling others, or their faith. I do not say that I have lived up to their examples, but I think their examples have lifted me to a higher place than before.

The hardest part is always putting all this "into practice" (vs. 9). The only way of learning any skill, trade, or sport is by practicing. Paul encourages his readers to put into practice what he has taught them. We must practice avoiding quarrels and staying united with other Christians. We must practice avoiding worry and anxiety by bringing everything to the Lord in prayer. We must practice thinking about the good things. We must practice what we see in the lives of godly men and women. If we do, then Paul promises that "the God of peace" will be with us (vs. 9).

Unforgiveness and quarreling cut us off from God; worry cuts us off from God; sinful thoughts cut us off from God; following bad examples cut us off from God. But forgiveness, unity, prayer, thankfulness, right thinking, and following good examples keep us close to the God of peace. As we watch our relationship with God and with others, as we watch our thoughts and the example of others, we can be confident that we will "stand firm in the Lord" and that in ten years—or twenty or thirty or fifty—and into eternity we will still be walking in a close relationship with the God of peace.

9 New Generosity

PHILIPPIANS 4:10-23

[10]I rejoice greatly in the Lord that at last you have renewed your concern for me. Indeed, you have been concerned, but you had no opportunity to show it. [11]I am not saying this because I am in need, for I have learned to be content whatever the circumstances. [12]I know what it is to be in need, and I know what it is to have plenty. I have learned the secret of being content in any and every situation, whether well fed or hungry, whether living in plenty or in want. [13]I can do everything through him who gives me strength.

[14]Yet it was good for you to share in my troubles. [15]Moreover, as you Philippians know, in the early days of your acquaintance with the gospel, when I set out from Macedonia, not one church shared with me in the matter of giving and receiving, except you only; [16]for even when I was in Thessalonica, you sent me aid again and again when I was in need. [17]Not that I am looking for a gift, but I am looking for what may be credited to your account. [18]I have received full payment and even more; I am amply supplied, now that I have received from Epaphroditus the gifts you sent. They are a fragrant offering, an acceptable sacrifice, pleasing to God. [19]And my God will meet all your needs according to his glorious riches in Christ Jesus.

[20]To our God and Father be glory for ever and ever. Amen.

[21]Greet all the saints in Christ Jesus. The brothers who are with me send greetings. [22]All the saints send you greetings, especially those who belong to Caesar's household.

[23]The grace of the Lord Jesus Christ be with your spirit. Amen.

When the issue of money and giving is raised in the context of the Christian faith, one of two pictures often comes to mind. First, people think of the American TV evangelists. I heard of one who had wires connected to the seats in his church. "All those who are willing to give one hundred dollars to God," he shouted, "stand up!" As he said this, he pressed a button and electricity zapped through the seats. There was a tremendous response, but later the ushers found three dead Scotsmen clinging to their pews! (Please don't be offended if you are a Scot. I, too, have some Scots blood!)

The other picture that comes to mind is desperately searching for loose change as the collection plate is passed during the last hymn. "The huge, brass offertory plates were passed around the congregation one Sunday evening—and returned almost empty to the vicar. He took them, held them up to heaven and prayed, 'Lord, we thank you for the safe return of these plates . . . '"41

The picture Paul paints in Philippians 4 is quite different from either of these. He writes to thank this group of Christians at Philippi who have sent him money via Epaphroditus. In a passage that includes two of the most wonderful promises in the Bible, he outlines the threefold blessing of generous giving.

GENEROUS GIVING BRINGS JOY TO OTHERS (VSS. 10-16)

Paul thanks the Philippians for making him so happy. He writes: "I rejoice greatly in the Lord that at last you have renewed your concern for me. Indeed, you have been concerned, but you had no opportunity to show it" (vs. 10). In the next verses he reveals his attitude to money.

On the one hand, Paul writes that in some ways he does not need the money. "I am not saying this because I am in need" (vs. 11). Why has he no need? Because he has learned something very important. Elsewhere he tells the Christians in Rome that before he was a Christian, he used to be envious of others and covetous

(Romans 7:8). Now he has "learned to be content whatever the circumstances. I know what it is to be in need, and I know what it is to have plenty. I have learned the secret of being content in any and every situation, whether well fed or hungry, whether living in plenty or in want" (vss. 11, 12).

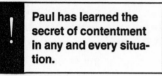

Paul has learned the secret of contentment in any and every situation.

As Martin Luther once said, "Contentment is a rare bird, but it sings sweetly in the breast."

What is the secret of contentment? Many think that the secret is to have everything they want. They say to themselves, "If only I had a better house, a bigger car, more money ... then I would be content." Others think the secret lies in human relationships or in looking beautiful. The singer George Michael achieved all this, but it did not bring contentment, as he explained in his song "Freedom '90": "I was every little hungry schoolgirl's pride and joy," he wrote. He had "brand new clothes and a big fat place." But, he concluded, "Sometimes the clothes do not make the man."[42]

These things do not bring contentment, only a desire for more of the same. John D. Rockefeller, who founded the Standard Oil Company and made hundreds of millions of dollars, was once asked, "How much money does it take to make a man happy?" He answered, "Just a little bit more than he has."

Paul has learned to be content in any and every situation. He is not saying there is anything wrong with having food and possessions, but these should not be the primary source of our contentment. Nor should they become gods.

For Paul the secret of real contentment is the transforming friendship of Jesus Christ. He writes, "I can do everything through him who gives me strength" (vs. 13). He has learned to live not on his outer resources, but on his inner resources. The person who has learned this secret is truly rich. Benjamin Franklin once said, "Content makes poor men rich; discontent makes rich men poor." Paul was rich because, in Christ, he had found the secret of contentment. For this reason he was able to write to the Philippians that in some ways he did not need their money.

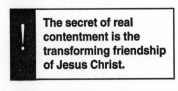

The secret of real contentment is the transforming friendship of Jesus Christ.

However, in some ways he did need the money. He writes:

> Yet it was good of you to share in my troubles. Moreover, as you Philippians know, in the early days of your acquaintance with the gospel, when I set out from Macedonia, not one church shared with me in the matter of giving and receiving, except you only; for even when I was in Thessalonica, you sent me aid again and again when I was in need (vss. 14-16).

Paul had had troubles and had been "in need." The Philippians had shared in his troubles and sent him money again and again. The word used for "share" is a word derived from the Greek word *koinonia*, which means fellowship, communion, or close relationship. It is a favorite expression for the marital relationship as the most intimate between human beings. Sharing is a vital part of life with those with whom we have a close relationship.

In the church, sharing should take place spontaneously in order to meet all its needs so that the entire burden does not fall on a few, and so that the needs of the less well off can be met. This is the way of bringing blessing to individuals who, like Paul, are in need, and blessing to the church that has its needs met also. As we share in giving, we also share in the blessing that accrues to the receiver. That is one of the reasons why giving is a blessing to the giver as well as to the receiver.

GENEROUS GIVING BRINGS JOY TO THOSE WHO GIVE (VSS. 17-18)

Paul does not want the Philippians to think that he is asking them for money. He is more concerned that they should be blessed.

All through this passage, Paul uses technical banking and accounting terms. In verse 15 he speaks of credit and debit (giving and receiving, the two sides of an accountant's ledger. In verse 17 he writes about profit and interest. The word for "credited" is a word used in banking for financial growth. Finally, in verse 18 when he says, "I have received

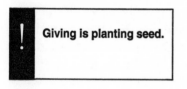

Giving is planting seed.

full payment," he uses a commercial term meaning "to receive a sum in full and give a receipt for it."[43]

Putting it into commercial terms, Paul explains that giving is an investment of capital. Elsewhere he uses the picture of a farmer sowing seed: "Remember this: Whoever sows sparingly will also reap sparingly, and whoever sows generously will also reap generously" (2 Corinthians 9:6). Giving is planting seed. A farmer who sows is investing for the future, for he knows that he will reap far more than he has sown.

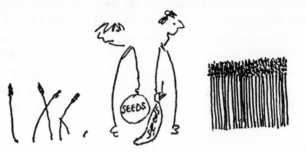

Hudson Taylor (1832-1905) founded the China Inland Mission. Thousands were converted through his ministry. It is said that he laid the foundations for the present revival in China, in which millions are turning to Jesus Christ. At the age of twenty-seven he was preparing to go to China. He was working hard during the week and ministering on Sundays. He lived a very frugal life. He ate a bowl of porridge in the morning and a bowl of gruel on alternate nights.

One day Taylor was asked to go and pray for a poor man and his wife, who was dying. The only money he possessed in the world was a half-crown piece—his week's wages. When he saw their poverty, he wanted to give. He said that if he had had two shillings and a sixpence he would have given the shilling. When he saw the poverty of the mother and the five children, he felt he would gladly have given one shilling and

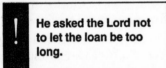

> He asked the Lord not to let the loan be too long.

sixpence. As he talked about the love of the heavenly Father, he felt he was a hypocrite, as he was not prepared to trust God without two shillings and sixpence. At this stage, he would gladly have given two shillings and kept sixpence.

Eventually, Taylor responded to their request for prayer and started to pray, "Our Father ... " He struggled through the Lord's Prayer. The husband said, "If you can help us, for God's sake, do." After an immense struggle, he gave them the only money he possessed in the world, the half crown piece. Joy flooded his heart. He sang all the way home. As he ate his gruel that night, Taylor reminded the Lord that "he that giveth to the poor, lendeth to the Lord." He asked the Lord not to let the loan be a long one. He slept peacefully.

The following morning Taylor received an unexpected letter. Inside he found a pair of gloves and half a sovereign. He had received a four hundred percent return on his investment in twelve hours. The incident was a turning point in Hudson Taylor's life. He came back to it time and again. He had learned to trust God in the little things, and it helped him in the more serious trials of life.

This spiritual principle applies to everything in life. Whatever we give to the Lord, He multiplies, whether it is our time, gifts, ambitions, or money. The return on our investment is not necessarily financial; rather, we are investing in people. We see lives changed, people coming into the kingdom of God, the hungry being fed, the naked clothed, drug addicts set free, marriages restored, and the sick healed. Every time we hear a good report about work in which we have invested, we are reaping the reward for our investment. For the most part, we will have to wait until heaven to see the harvest, but we get occasional glimpses of it here and now, as a foretaste.

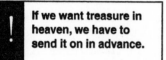

! If we want treasure in heaven, we have to send it on in advance.

The New Testament principle is that if we want treasure in heaven, we have to send it on in advance. What will the reward in heaven be? I don't know, but I suspect we will see the faces of those we have unknowingly helped. We will hear them say, "I became a

Christian partly as a result of your gift," or, "My marriage was restored," or, "I was healed." Not only will we see their faces, but we will see the face of Jesus. We get a foretaste of this now, which is why in giving generously it is not only the recipients who are blessed, we also are blessed.

GENEROUS GIVING BRINGS JOY TO GOD (VSS. 18B-19)

Paul now turns from the commercial world of banking to the language of the temple. He writes that such a mundane matter as a material gift is first of all a "fragrant offering" (vs. 18). This language is borrowed from the Old Testament and means literally "the fragrance of a sweet smell." It is the expression used for Christ's offering of Himself for us on the cross (Ephesians 5:2). It speaks of something very beautiful, an act of great love.

Second, generous giving is "an acceptable sacrifice" (vs. 18). We cannot earn our salvation. The sacrifice of Jesus was "a full, perfect, and sufficient sacrifice."[44] We cannot add to something that is already full, perfect, and sufficient. Our sacrifice is one of thanksgiving and praise, and part of that should be a generosity in our giving. It may be a sacrifice, and sacrifices are not always easy. There is a cost: it is hard to give; it goes against the grain. Yet it is an act which, more than anything else, liberates us from the hold money might otherwise have on our lives.

> **!** Our sacrifice is one of thanksgiving and praise.

Third, Paul says that generous giving is "pleasing to God" (vs. 18). It is an extraordinary and wonderful assertion of the New Testament generally—and in particular of Paul in this passage—that what we do here can please God. If we give generously to His children, God is pleased.

Throughout the New Testament we are encouraged to give generously. Our giving should be regular ("on the first day of every week"—1 Corinthians 16:2). It should be proportionate to our income ("each one of you should set aside a sum of money in keeping with his income"—2 Corinthians 16:2). Jacob the swindler gave one tenth, Zacchaeus the tax collector gave half, the devout Jew gave a sixth. Many Christians believe it is right to give a tenth (on the basis of Matthew 23:23). These may be guidelines, but generosity is the only rule in the New Testament. As we give generously, Paul says: "My God will meet all your needs according to his glorious riches in Christ Jesus" (vs. 19).

It is very personal—Paul speaks of "my God." Paul can trust God because his is a close, personal, intimate relationship with God. God will meet "all your needs." The word means "fill up by adding."

God promises to meet "all your needs."

Many Christians who give, say, ten percent of their income, have found that the ninety percent left more than covers what the one hundred did before they started giving. God promises to meet "all your needs." This must include our material needs (though not necessarily our material *wants*). Our needs will be met "according to his glorious riches in Christ Jesus"— not merely from His wealth, but in a manner that befits His wealth. We cannot out-give God.

Our generosity stems from God's generosity to us. It is no coincidence that the letter to the Philippians begins and ends with grace (Philippians 1:2; 4:23), for at the heart of this letter we see God's grace expounded. "Grace" is one of the most important words in the New Testament. It summarizes the essence of Christianity. It includes all the riches of God's undeserved love for us, made possible through the life, death, and resurrection of Jesus Christ. The central theme of

113

this letter is the central theme of the New Testament and the Bible as a whole: God's love and generosity.

God's love and generosity are seen throughout the Bible, and supremely in the cross of Christ. Jesus taught that our highest duty is to love God with all our hearts, souls, and minds. After that, our duty is to love our neighbor as ourselves (Matthew 22:37-40). In the last four verses of Philippians, we see examples of such love that also summarize so much of the teaching in the book.

First, Paul expresses his *love for God.* Paul loves the one who is both his God and Father and theirs. His overriding desire is to see God's name glorified (vs. 20). He ends this section with a tribute of praise that "comes as a splendid climax, and 'flows from the joy of the whole epistle' i.e., it is Paul's fitting response, borrowed from the liturgical practice of the primitive churches, to all the things which cause him joy in his prison experience."[45]

Second, he expresses his *love for others.* In the final verses Paul sends his greetings to each one of God's people (vs. 21). He wants to make sure that they all hear that he sends his love to them. And he points out that it is not only him, but "all the saints send you greetings" (vs. 22). He sends special greetings from the Christian brothers who belong to Caesar's household—the government administration in Rome, a kind of imperial civil service. Christianity had already penetrated the highest positions in the Empire. "The crucified Galilean carpenter had already begun to rule those who ruled the greatest empire in the world."[46]

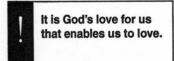

It is God's love for us that enables us to love.

Third, Paul ends as he began, with *God's undeserved love for us.* Jesus is the channel of all the good gifts that come to us. Paul prays for "The grace of the Lord Jesus Christ" (vs. 23) to be with the

Philippians. It is His love for us that enables us to love Him and to love others. He is the source of our love. I think that if we asked Paul for a two-word answer to the question, "Why is life worth living?" he would reply, "Jesus Christ."

Notes

1. J .B. Lightfoot, *St. Paul's Epistle to the Philippians*, 1st ed. (Zondervan, 1868), p. 55.
2. William Barclay, *The Daily Study Bible, The Letters to the Philippians, Colossians and Thessalonians* (The Saint Andrew Press, 1975), p. 57.
3. J. B. Lightfoot, *St. Paul's Epistle to the Philippians*, 1st ed. (Zondervan, 1868), p. 57.
4. Ibid., p. 85.
5. Malcolm Muggeridge, *Conversion—A Spiritual Journey* (Harper Collins, 1988), p. 135.
6. Jonathan Goforth, *When the Spirit's Fire Swept Korea* (Zondervan, 1943), pp. 190, 191.
7. Ralph P. Martin, *Philippians*, Tyndale New Testament Commentaries (InterVarsity Press, 1959), p. 68.
8. Martin Wroe, ed., *God: What the Critics Say* (Spire, 1992), p. 16.
9. John Stott, *Issues Facing Christians Today* (Marshall Pickering 1984), p. 67.
10. Gore Vidal, *Daily Mail*, September 12, 1992, Solo.
11. Gore Vidal, *Sunday Times Magazine*, September 16, 1973.
12. William Barclay, *The Daily Study Bible, The Letters to the Philippians, Colossians and Thessalonians* (The Saint Andrew Press, 1975), p. 32.
13. William Temple, *Christianity and Social Order* (SCM Press, 1950), pp. 49, 50.
14. Alec Motyer, *The Message of Philippians* (InterVarsity Press, 1984), p. 131.
15. John Stott, *The Contemporary Christian* (InterVarsity Press, 1992), p. 47.

16. Ibid., p. 53.
17. George Bernard Shaw, *Liberty* (Oxford Dictionary of Quotations).
18. Alec Motyer, *The Message of Philippians* (InterVarsity Press, 1984), p. 127.
19. *The Times*, November 21, 1992.
20. Stephen Gaukroger and Nick Mercer, *Frogs in Cream* (Scripture Union, 1990), p. 124.
21. J. B. Lightfoot, *St. Paul's Epistle to the Philippians*, 1st ed. (Zondervan, 1868), p. 117.
22. *The Times*, November 16, 1992.
23. C. S. Lewis, *The Four Loves* (Geoffrey Bles Ltd, Harper Collins, 1960), pp. 69–70.
24. W. E. Gladstone, *Quotable Quotations* (Victor Books, 1985), p. 345.
25. Dale Carnegie, *How to Win Friends and Influence People* (Cedar Press, 1953), p. 73.
26. C. S. Lewis, *The Four Loves* (Geoffrey Bles Ltd., Harper Collins, 1960), p. 79.
27. J. B. Lightfoot, *St. Paul's Epistle to the Philippians* (Zondervan, 1868), p. 123.
28. James Dobson, *Preparing for Adolescence* (Kingsway, 1982).
29. Madonna, *Vanity Fair*, April 1991.
30. Alec Motyer, *The Message of Philippians* (InterVarsity Press, 1984), p. 158.
31. John T. McNeill, ed., *John Calvin's, Institutes of the Christian Religion*, Book II, 16.6 (Westminster Press, 1960).
32. G. E. Ladd, *New Testament Theology* (Lutterworth Press, 1974), p. 449.
33. Joanna and Alister McGrath, *The Dilemma of Self-Esteem* (Crossway Books, 1992), p. 134.
34. John Dillenberger, ed., *Martin Luther: Selections from His Writings* (Anchor Books, 1961), pp. 10-12.

35. John Stott, *Christ the Controversialist* (InterVarsity Press, 1970), p. 192.

36. Alec Motyer, *The Message of Philippians* (InterVarsity Press, 1984), p. 169.

37. J. B. Lightfoot, *St. Paul's Epistle to the Philippians,* 1st ed. (Zondervan, 1868), p. 151.

38. Charles W. Colson, *Born Again* (Hodder & Stoughton, 1976), pp. 34, 62, 272.

39. C. S. Lewis, *The Weight of Glory* (Macmillan, 1980), p. 18.

40. J. B. Lightfoot, op. cit., p. 106.

41. Gaukroger & Mercer, *Frogs in Cream* (Scripture Union, 1990), p. 116.

42. George Michael, "Freedom '90" (*Listen without Prejudice,* Vol. I).

43. William F. Arndt and F. Wilbur Gingrich, *Walter Bauer's Greek English Lexicon of the New Testament,* 2nd. ed. (University of Chicago Press, 1979)

44. *The Book of Common Prayer* (W. M. Collins & Co Ltd).

45. Ralph P. Martin, *The New Century Bible Commentary, Philippians* (Marshall, Morgan & Scott Ltd, 1976), p. 169.

46. William Barclay, *The Daily Study Bible, The Letters to the Philippians, Colossians and Thessalonians* (The Saint Andrew Press, 1975), p. 87.

A LIFE WORTH LIVING

Study Guide

BY DAVID STONE

The following study questions are intended to help you get to the heart of what the author has written and challenge you to apply what you learn to your own life. The questions can be used by individuals or by small groups meeting together.

1. NEW HEART (PHILIPPIANS 1:3-11)

A heart of confidence

1. " … as so often happens when circumstances seem against us, God opened up something much better" (p. 15). What experience have you had of this? Why do you think God works in this way?

2. To get a feel for the background to what Paul writes to the Philippians, read the story of what happened to him at Philippi in Acts 16:11-40. What do you notice from Luke's account?

3. How does Paul know that it is God who "began a good work" in the lives of the Christians at Philippi (p. 16)?

4. "He who began a good work in you will carry it on to completion until the day of Christ Jesus." What does this imply for your future?

5. What is the "hallmark of the Christian" (p. 17)? Do you know anyone like Nicky's friend Henry? How might you pray for them?

A heart of compassion

6. Paul "knew how to be tough, but he also knew how to be tender" (p. 18). What evidence is there for this statement? How are we to work out which is the right approach in any given situation?

7. Why must love be "the motivating force behind … ministry" p. 19)? What happens when it isn't? What experience have you had of this?

8. Where does such love come from? How?

A heart of concern

9. How can we assess the health of a church (p. 20 and following)? How healthy is yours? Why? In what ways could you make a positive contribution?

10. In what way is Christian love to be "more than an emotional experience" (p. 21)? How in practice can it be so for you?
11. Is there anything about you that might be a "barrier to God's blessing"—either in your life or in your church (p. 23)? What can you do about it?

Consider how you might pray for these three aspects of what it means to have a "new heart."

2. NEW PURPOSE (PHILIPPIANS 1:12-30)

1. From what Paul says, what is it that enables him to make light of his sufferings to the point of rejoicing in them (p. 26 and following)? To what extent do you share his perspective?
2. Is there any way in which you "feel trapped" and unable to serve Christ as you would ideally like to (p. 28)? How do Paul's words help?
3. In what ways do you "speak the word of God" (p. 28)? Is there scope for you to do so "more courageously and fearlessly"? How might this be possible?
4. "Sometimes people refrain from doing what is right because they are worried about their motives" (p. 29). Are there situations where this is true of you? What do you think Paul would say?
5. How do you react to people who appear to be preaching the Gospel "for money or self-aggrandizement" (p. 30)? Would Paul agree with you?
6. Why need Christians have no worries about death (p. 30 and following)? Do you share Paul's outlook on this?
7. What drives Paul (p. 31 and following)? What drives you? How do you know?
8. How does an appreciation of Roman customs help us to understand what Paul is talking about in Philippians 1 (p. 33 and following)?
9. In what ways does the enemy "seek to divide" you from other Christians (p. 34)? What can you do to thwart his strategy?

3. NEW ATTITUDE (PHILIPPIANS 2:1-11)

1. What arguments does Paul use as the basis of his appeal for Christian unity (p. 36 and following)?
2. How does Philippians 2:2 help us to understand exactly what unity means (p. 37)?
3. With whom should you be united in the way Paul describes? Are you?
4. What wrong attitudes does Paul identify that are likely to undermine unity (p. 37 and following)?
5. How prevalent are wrong attitudes—both in society generally and in your own life?
6. In what ways does "the mind of Christ" differ from what would be expected of humanity in general (p. 41 and following)?
7. What is "the great glory of Christian ethics" (p. 43)? How does this work out in practice for you?
8. How does Paul's teaching on true greatness challenge you (p. 43 and following)?
9. What is it that Nicky describes as "the extraordinary paradox of the Christian life" (p . 44)? Have you found this to be true? In what ways?

4. NEW RESPONSIBILITIES (PHILIPPIANS 2:12-18)

1. What does Paul mean by telling his readers to "work out your salvation with fear and trembling" (p. 48 and following)? Have you applied this to your own life? In what ways?

2. What does the word "salvation" mean (p. 48)? Why might it qualify as "the most important word in the New Testament"?

3. How do you react to the possibility of having "a saved soul and a wasted life" (p. 50)? How do you think Paul would advise someone who felt that this description applied to them?

4. What is the "very careful balance in Paul's wording" in Philippians 2:12, 13 (p. 51)? Why is this so important?

5. Why do many people "fear to trust God with their futures" (p. 51)? Why are such fears groundless?

6. What is "crooked and depraved" about modern society (p. 51 and following)? In what ways is the situation different today from that in the past?

7. In what ways should the lives of Christians be "noticeably different from those around them" (p. 52)? Have you met anyone whose attitude was noticeably different? Did you feel challenged? In what way?

8. What does it mean to "hold out the word of life" (p. 53 and following)? How do you go about doing this?

9. How can we maintain ourselves in "peak condition spiritually" (p. 54)? Who suffers if we are not at our best for God?

10. "Ministry is pouring ourselves out for others" (p. 55). In what ways have you experienced this?

11. How should we pray for those who feel weighed down and "in need of recharging" (p. 55)?

5. NEW FRIENDSHIPS (PHILIPPIANS 2:19-30)

1. How do you react to the author's claim that "friendship is at the heart of Christianity" (p. 58)? Is it at the heart of yours?

2. Why is it that we "desire and need close human friendships" (pp. 58, 59), and yet find them so hard? What difference does Christianity make to this situation?

3. In what way is friendship "even more important than marriage" (p. 59)? Who are your friends?

4. What mark of Timothy's genuine friendship does Paul focus on in Philippians 2:20 (p. 60 and following)? How does such an attitude come about?

5. What is "by far the most effective way to pass on the Good News of Jesus Christ" (pp. 61, 62)? What experience have you had of this?

6. Do you agree that Christian friendship is "in a different league" from ordinary friendship (p. 62)? What makes such friendships work?

7. How can we prevent Christian fellowship from becoming too inward looking (p. 63 and following)? What can you do to put this into practice in your own context?

8. What does the author describe as "the only real basis for a flourishing church" (p. 64)? How does this tie in with your own experience?

9. What "very real opposition" do we face as Christians (p. 64 and following)? In what practical ways can we help and be helped by one another?

10. "All friendship involves taking risks" (p. 66). In what ways have you found this to be true?

11. How should we pray for people who may be feeling particularly vulnerable as a result of things going wrong in their Christian friendships?

6. NEW CONFIDENCE (PHILIPPIANS 3:1-11)

1. How would you define self-confidence as opposed to over-confidence (p. 69 and following)?

False confidence

2. What exactly are the people described by Paul in Philippians 3:2 doing (p. 71 and following)? Why is Paul so incensed about it? Can you think of any equivalents in the church today?
3. " ... baptism ... is not enough" (p. 72). Why? And if so, then what value does it have?
4. In what do people try to put their confidence (p. 72 and following)? What makes these things inadequate?
5. What personal achievements does Paul draw attention to (p. 74 and following)? What parallels do you notice in your life?

True confidence

6. Where does Paul's new confidence come from (p. 76 and following)? How has his attitude changed? What do you think are the causes of such a dramatic change?
7. How is it possible for us "to be in a right relationship with God" (pp. 76, 77)? Is this something you have entered into? How did this happen?
8. What is "the great difference between false and true confidence" (p. 78)?
9. What steps can we take to help our confidence grow (p. 79)?

7. NEW AMBITIONS (PHILIPPIANS 3:10-21)

1. Would you describe yourself as ambitious (pp. 81, 82)? What makes you as you are in this respect?

Jesus-centered ambition

2. Do you "know Christ" (p. 83 and following)? What exactly does this mean?
3. Have you noticed the Holy Spirit bringing "resurrection power" to your life (p. 83)? In what ways?
4. What did it mean for Paul to share in the sufferings of Christ (p. 83 and following)? What does it mean for you? How do Paul's words help us to cope with such suffering?
5. What does it mean to be "ambitious for Christ" (p. 85)? Are you? Are there things that hold you back?

Man-centered ambition

6. What do Paul's tears in Philippians 3:18 tell us about him (p. 87)? What makes you weep? Why?
7. "Many people's lives revolve directly or indirectly around satisfying their bodily desires" (p. 89). Do you think this is true? What does Paul identify as the inevitable result of this attitude to life? Why?
8. "In this passage Paul tells us that everyone is on one of two paths" (p. 91). How do you respond to this?

8. NEW RESOURCES (PHILIPPIANS 4:1-9)

1. Where do you think you will be in ten years time (p. 93)?
2. In what ways do you find you need to "hold off the enemy" (p. 94)?
3. Why is unity within the church so important (p. 95)? What experience have you had of the consequences of divisions and splits?
4. In the light of what Paul says about Euodia and Syntyche, what do you think should be done when personality clashes occur (p. 95 and following)?
5. How can we ensure that the Lord really is our "chief ground of rejoicing" (p. 98)?
6. What makes the fact that the Lord is near a "reason for forbearance" (p. 98)? Are you aware of any situations where this is especially relevant for you at the moment?
7. "Prayer and worry are not easy bedfellows" (p. 99). Why not? What practical tips about prayer does Paul give?
8. What experiences have you had of "the peace of God, which transcends all understanding" of which Paul speaks in Philippians 4:7 (p. 99)?
9. "What we think is more important than who we are and what we have" (p. 100). Why?
10. Given the climate of the modern world, how can we put Philippians 4:8 into practice? Try to be specific.
11. How would you feel if others modeled themselves on your example (p. 101)?
12. How should we choose our role models?

9. NEW GENEROSITY (PHILIPPIANS 4:10-23)

1. What comes to your mind when "the issue of money and giving is raised in the context of the Christian faith"(p. 106)? Why?

2. What is the "secret of contentment" that Paul has discovered (p. 107)? Have you discovered it too?

3. Whom do you and your church "share with" in the way Paul describes (p. 108 and following)?

4. In what way is giving "an investment of capital" (p. 109 and following)? What sort of return can we expect? Why?

5. What is "the New Testament principle" by which we gain treasure in heaven (p. 111)? In what ways are you putting this into practice?

6. How does God react to generous giving (p. 112 and following)? Why?

7. What practical steps can we take to ensure that our giving is generous (pp. 112, 113)?

8. "We cannot out-give God" (p. 113). Have you found this to be true? In what ways?

9. How would Paul answer the question, "Why is life worth living?" (p. 115)? How would you answer it?

Alpha Resources

This book is an *Alpha* resource. The *Alpha Course* is a practical introduction to the Christian faith developed by Holy Trinity Brompton Church in London, England. *Alpha Courses* are now being run worldwide.

Resources needed for setting up the *Alpha Course* (training)

- The *Alpha Course* Introductory Video
- *Alpha* Conference Tapes OR • How to Run *Alpha* Video Set
- *Alpha* Leader's Training Tapes or Videos (set of 3 talks)
- The *Alpha Course* Leader's Guide (one for each small-group leader and helper)

Resources needed for running the *Alpha Course*

- The *Alpha Course* Tapes OR
- The *Alpha Course* Videos (5-video set including 15 talks)
- The *Alpha Course* Manual (one for each small-group participant and leader)
- The *Alpha Course* Leader's Guide (one for each small-group leader and helper)
- Registration Brochures (one for each potential participant; sold in packets of 50)
- *Why Jesus?* (recommended reading for each participant)
- *Questions of Life* (recommended reading for each leader and participant)
- *Searching Issues* (recommended reading for each leader and participant)

Alpha Books BY NICKY GUMBEL

Why Jesus? A booklet recommended for all participants at the start of the *Alpha Course.*

Why Christmas? The Christmas version of *Why Jesus?*

Questions of Life The *Alpha Course* in book form. In fifteen compelling chapters the author points the way to an authentic Christianity which is exciting and relevant to today's world.

Searching Issues Seven issues most often raised by participants of the *Alpha Course:* suffering, other religions, sex before marriage, the New Age, homosexuality, science & Christianity, and the Trinity.

A Life Worth Living What happens after *Alpha?* Based on the book of Philippians, this is an invaluable next step for those who have just completed the *Alpha Course,* and for anyone eager to put their faith on a firm biblical footing.

Challenging Lifestyle An in-depth look at the Sermon on the Mount (Matthew 5–7). The author shows that Jesus' teaching flies in the face of modern lifestyle and presents us with a radical alternative.

Telling Others This book includes the principles and practicalities of setting up and running an *Alpha Course.* It also includes personal accounts of lives changed while attending an *Alpha Course.*

30 Days Nicky Gumbel selects 30 passages from the Old and New Testament which can be read over 30 days. It is designed for those taking an Alpha course and others who are interested in beginning to explore the Bible.

The Heart of Revival Ten Bible studies based on the book of Isaiah, drawing out important truths for today by interpreting some of the teaching of the Old Testament prophet Isaiah. The book seeks to understand what revival might mean and how we can prepare to be part of it.

In North America, all *Alpha* resources are published by Cook Ministry Resources, a division of Cook Communications Ministries.

In the USA, call or write:

Cook Ministry Resources
4050 Lee Vance View
Colorado Springs, CO 80918-7100
1-800-426-6596
1-800-36-ALPHA (1-800-362-5742)

In Canada, call or write:

Beacon Distributing
P.O. Box 98
55 Woodslee Ave.
Paris Ontario N3L 3E5
1-800-263-2664

All books are also available from your local Christian bookstore.